Eureka Math Study Guide

Other Books

WHEATLEY PORTFOLIO

English, Grades K–5, Second Edition

English, Grades 6–8, Second Edition

English, Grades 9–12, Second Edition

ALEXANDRIA PLAN

United States History, Grades K–2

World History, Grades K–2

United States History, Grades 3–5

World History, Grades 3–5

Eureka Math Study Guide
Grade 5

Published by Jossey-Bass
A Wiley Brand
One Montgomery Street, Suite 1000, San Francisco, CA 94104-4594–www.josseybass.com

Jossey-Bass books and products are available through most bookstores. To contact Jossey-Bass directly, call our Customer Care Department within the U.S. at 800-956-7739, outside the U.S. at 317-572-3986, or fax 317-572-4002.

For more information about Eureka Math, visit www.eureka-math.org.

Wiley publishes in a variety of print and electronic formats and by print-on-demand. Some material included with standard print versions of this book may not be included in e-books or in print-on-demand. If this book refers to media such as a CD or DVD that is not included in the version you purchased, you may download this material at http://booksupport.wiley.com. For more information about Wiley products, visit www.wiley.com.

Library of Congress Cataloging-in-Publication Data

Eureka math study guide. A story of units, grade 5 education edition / Great Minds–First edition.
    pages   cm
  Includes bibliographical references and index.
  ISBN 978-1-118-81181-8 (paperback)
  1. Mathematics–Study and teaching (Preschool)–Standards–United States.   I. Great Minds
QA135.6.E83 2015
372.7'2–dc23
                                                                    2014029344

Printed in the United States of America

FIRST EDITION
PB Printing 10 9 8 7 6 5 4 3 2 1

Contents

Introduction

When do you know you really understand something? One test is to see if you can explain it to someone else—well enough that *they* understand it. *Eureka Math* routinely requires students to "turn and talk" and explain the math they learned to their peers.

That is because the goal of *Eureka Math* (which you may know as the EngageNY math modules) is to produce students who are not merely literate, but fluent, in mathematics. By fluent, we mean not just knowing what process to use when solving a problem but understanding why that process works.

Here's an example. A student who is fluent in mathematics can do far more than just name, recite, and apply the Pythagorean theorem to problems. She can explain why $a^2 + b^2 = c^2$ is true. She not only knows the theorem can be used to find the length of a right triangle's hypotenuse, but can apply it more broadly—such as to find the distance between any two points in the coordinate plane, for example. She also can see the theorem as the glue joining seemingly disparate ideas including equations of circles, trigonometry, and vectors.

By contrast, the student who has merely memorized the Pythagorean theorem does not know why it works and can do little more than just solve right triangle problems by rote. The theorem is an abstraction—not a piece of knowledge, but just a process to use in the limited ways that she has been directed. For her, studying mathematics is a chore, a mere memorizing of disconnected processes.

Eureka Math provides much more. It offers students math knowledge that will serve them well beyond any test. This fundamental knowledge not only makes wise citizens and competent consumers, but it gives birth to budding physicists and engineers. Knowing math deeply opens vistas of opportunity.

A student becomes fluent in math—as they do in any other subject—by following a course of study that builds their knowledge of the subject, logically and thoroughly. In *Eureka Math*, concepts flow logically from PreKindergarten through high school. The "chapters" in the story of mathematics are "A Story of Units" for the elementary grades, followed by "A Story of Ratios" in middle school and "A Story of Functions" in high school.

This sequencing is joined with a mix of new and old methods of instruction that are proven to work. For example, we utilize an exercise called a "sprint" to develop students' fluency with standard algorithms (routines for adding, subtracting, multiplying, and dividing whole numbers and fractions). We employ many familiar models and tools such as the number line and tape diagrams (aka bar models). A newer model highlighted in the curriculum is the number bond (illustrated below), which clearly shows how numbers are comprised of other numbers.

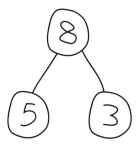

Eureka Math is designed to help accommodate different types of classrooms and serve as a resource for educators, who make decisions based on the needs of students. The "vignettes" of teacher-student interactions included in the curriculum are not scripts, but exemplars illustrating methods of instruction recommended by the teachers who have crafted our curricula.

Eureka Math has been adopted by districts from East Meadows, New York, to Lafayette, Los Angeles, to Chula Vista, California. At *Eureka Math* we are excited to have created the most transparent math curriculum in history—every lesson, all classwork, and every problem is available online.

Many of us have less than joyful memories of learning mathematics: lots of memorization, lots of rules to follow without understanding, and problems that didn't make any sense. What if a curriculum came along that gave children a chance to avoid that math anxiety and replaced it with authentic understanding, excitement, and curiosity? Like a New York educator attending one of our trainings said: "Why didn't I learn mathematics this way when I was a kid? It is so much easier than the way I learned it!"

Eureka!

Lynne Munson
Washington, DC

From the Writers

To My Fellow Teachers:

As a young child, I was captivated by the steadiness, security, and beauty of mathematics. Whether I was checking the baseball box scores or learning a new application of the Pythagorean Theorem, math provided me a source of confidence, understanding, and pleasure. As a teacher, I grew to treasure the sequential nature of mathematics instruction and loved watching my students grow in their understanding and application of new math concepts. I looked forward to diagnosing my students' misunderstandings and identifying the most efficient ways to remediate these misconceptions.

As a writer of the *Eureka Math* curriculum, I've learned to appreciate math in new ways and, more clearly than ever, recognize the powerful results that can be gained from content-rich mathematics instruction. And as a father, I'm thrilled when thinking about what an impact this curriculum could have on the education my children will receive.

Helping to write *Eureka*'s Grade 5 curriculum has been, by far, the most exciting project of my career. The new standards presented my colleagues and me, now close friends, with an ideal opportunity for twenty-first-century collaboration: we live in five different states yet developed the curriculum together. The level of thought, intentionality, and compassion devoted to each aspect of every lesson in A *Story of Units* is something that I have never witnessed before. Countless decisions were made about how best to reach students, whom we've never met and who are each thinking and operating on a multitude of levels. Perhaps you can imagine the uncertainty we all felt undertaking such a task. No doubt you know your students best and will want to study the curriculum carefully to make any adjustments necessary to meet their specific needs.

And so I—along with all those who wrote, critiqued, wrote again, revised, rewrote, and edited—give this gift to you! I can't wait to see it evolve in your classrooms as your passion, creativity, and intelligence guide you to customize the curriculum in an even richer and more rigorous manner to meet the demands of your students, your school, and your community.

Adam Baker
Marlboro, NY
Grade 5 lead writer/editor
Eureka Math/Great Minds

Foreword

TELLING THE STORY OF MATH

Each module in *Eureka Math* builds carefully and precisely on the content learned in the previous modules and years, weaving the knowledge learned into a coherent whole. This produces an effect similar to reading a good novel: The storyline, even after weeks of not reading, is easy to pick up again because the novel pulls the reader back into the plot immediately—the need to review is minimal because the plot brings out and adds to what has already happened. This cumulative aspect of the plot, along with its themes, character development, and composition, are all part of the carefully thought-out design of the *Eureka Math* curriculum.

So what is the storyline? One can get a sense of how the story evolves by studying the major themes of A *Story of Units*, A *Story of Ratios*, and A *Story of Functions*.

A *Story of Units* investigates how concepts including place value, algorithms, fractions, measurements, area, and so on can all be understood by relating and manipulating types of units (e.g., inches, square meters, tens, fifths). For example, quantities expressed in the same units can be added: 3 apples plus 4 apples equals 7 apples. Likewise, 3 fifths plus 4 fifths is 7 fifths. Whole number multiplication, as in "3 fives = 15 ones," is merely another form of converting between different units, as when we state that "1 foot = 12 inches." These similarities between concepts drive the day-to-day theme throughout the PreK–5 curriculum: each type of unit (or building block) is handled the same way through the common features that all units share. Understanding the commonalities and like traits of these building blocks makes it much easier to sharply contrast the differences. In other words, the consistency of manipulation of different units helps students see the connection in topics. No longer is every new topic separate from the previous topics studied.

A *Story of Ratios* moves students beyond problems that involve one-time calculations using one or two specific measurements to thinking about proportional relationships that hold for a whole range of measurements. The proportional relationships theme shows up every day during middle school as students work with ratios, rates, percentages, probability, similarity, and linear functions. A *Story of Ratios* provides the transition years between students thinking of a specific triangle with side lengths 3 cm, 4 cm, and 5 cm in elementary school to a broader view in high school for studying the set of all triangles with side lengths in a 3:4:5 ratio (e.g., 6:8:10, 9:12:15).

A *Story of Functions* generalizes linear relationships learned in middle school to polynomial, rational, trigonometric, exponential, and logarithmic functions in high school. Students study the properties of these functions and their graphs, and model with them to move explicitly from real-world scenarios to mathematical representations. The algebra learned in middle school is applied in rewriting functions in different forms and solving equations derived from one or more functions. The theme drives students to finish high school knowing not only how to manipulate the major functions used in college but also to be fully capable of modeling real-life data with an appropriate function in order to make predictions and answer questions.

The many "little eurekas" infused in the storyline of *Eureka Math* help students learn how to wield the true power of mathematics in their daily lives. Experiencing these "aha moments" also convinces students that the mathematics that drives innovation and advancement in our society is within their reach.

Scott Baldridge
Lead writer and lead mathematician, *Eureka Math*
Loretta Cox Stuckey and Dr. James G. Traynham Distinguished Professor of Mathematics,
Louisiana State University
Co-director, Gordon A. Cain Center for Science, Technology,
Engineering, and Mathematical Literacy

How to Use This Book

As a self-study resource, these *Eureka Math* Study Guides are beneficial for teachers in a variety of situations. They introduce teachers who are brand new to either the classroom or the *Eureka Math* curriculum not only to *Eureka Math* but also to the content of the grade level in a way they will find manageable and useful. Teachers already familiar with the curriculum will also find this resource valuable as it allows a meaningful study of the grade-level content in a way that highlights the connections between modules and topics. The guidebooks help teachers obtain a firm grasp on what it is that students should master during the year. The structure of the book provides a focus on the connections between the standards and the descriptions of mathematical progressions through the grade, topic by topic. Teachers therefore develop a multifaceted view of the standards from a thorough analysis of the guide.

The *Eureka Math* Study Guides can also serve as a means to familiarize teachers with adjacent grade levels. It is helpful for teachers to know what students learned in the grade level below the one they are currently teaching as well as the one that follows. Having an understanding of the mathematical progression across grades enhances the teacher's ability to reach students at their level and ensure they are prepared for the next grade.

For teachers, schools, and districts that have not adopted *Eureka Math*, but are instead creating or adjusting their own curricular frameworks, these grade-level study guides offer support in making critical decisions about how to group and sequence the standards for maximal coherence within and across grades. *Eureka Math* serves as a blueprint for these educators; in turn, the study guides present not only this blueprint but a rationale for the selected organization.

The *Eureka Math* model provides a starting point from which educators can build their own curricular plan if they so choose. Unpacking the new standards to determine what skills students should master at each grade level is a necessary exercise to ensure appropriate choices are made during curriculum development. The *Eureka Math* Study Guides include lists of student outcomes mapped to the standards and are key to the unpacking process. The overviews of the modules and topics offer narratives rich with detailed descriptions of how to teach specific skills needed at each grade level. Users can have confidence in the interpretations of the standards presented, as well as the sequencing selected, due to the rigorous review process that occurred during the development of the content included in *Eureka Math*.

This *Eureka Math* Study Guide contains the following:

Introduction to Eureka Math (chapter 1): This introduction consists of two sections: "Vision and Storyline" and "Advantages to a Coherent Curriculum."

Major Mathematical Themes in Each Grade Band (chapter 2): The first section presents year-long curriculum maps for each grade band (with subsections addressing *A Story of Units*, *A Story of Ratios*, and *A Story of Functions*). It is followed by a detailed examination of math concept development for PreK to Grade 5. The chapter closes with an in-depth description of how alignment to the Instructional Shifts and the Standards of Mathematical Practice is achieved.

Grade-Level Content Review (chapter 3): The key areas of focus and required fluencies for a given grade level are presented in this chapter, along with a rationale for why topics are grouped and sequenced in the modules as they are. The Alignment Chart lists the standards that are addressed in each module of the grade.

Curriculum Design (chapter 4): The approach to modules, lessons, and assessment in A *Story of Units* is detailed in this chapter. It also provides a wealth of information about how to achieve the components of instructional rigor demanded by the new standards: fluency, concept development, and application.

Approach to Differentiated Instruction (chapter 5): This chapter describes the approach to differentiated instruction used in A *Story of Units*. Special populations such as English language learners, students with disabilities, students performing above grade level, and students performing below grade level are addressed.

Grade-Level Module Summary and Unpacking of Standards (chapter 6): This chapter presents information from the modules to provide an overview of the content of each and explain the mathematical progression. The standards are translated for teachers, and a fuller picture is drawn of the teaching and learning that should take place through the school year.

Mathematical Models (chapter 7): This chapter presents information on the mathematical models used in A *Story of Units*.

Terminology (chapter 8): The terms included in this list were compiled from the New or Recently Introduced Terms portion of the Terminology section of the Module Overviews. Terms are listed by grade level and module number where they are introduced in A *Story of Units*. The chapter also offers descriptions, examples, and illustrations associated with the terms.

Eureka Math Study Guide

CHAPTER 1

Introduction to Eureka Math

VISION AND STORYLINE

Eureka Math is a comprehensive, content-rich PreK–12 curriculum and professional development platform. It follows the focus and coherence of the new college- and career-ready standards and carefully sequences the mathematical progressions into expertly crafted instructional modules.

The new standards and progressions set the frame for the curriculum. We then shaped every aspect of it by addressing the new instructional shifts that teachers must make. Nowhere are the instructional shifts more evident than in the fluency, application, concept development, and debriefing sections that characterize lessons in the PreK–5 grades of *Eureka Math*. Similarly, Eureka's focus in the middle and high school grades on problem sets, exploration, Socratic discussion, and modeling helps students internalize the true meaning of coherence and fosters deep conceptual understanding.

Eureka Math is distinguished not only by its adherence to the new standards, but also by its foundation in a theory of teaching math that has been proven to work. This theory posits that mathematical knowledge is conveyed most effectively when it is taught in a sequence that follows the story of mathematics itself. This is why we call the elementary portion A *Story of Units*, followed by A *Story of Ratios* in middle school, and A *Story of Functions* in high school. Mathematical concepts flow logically from one to the next in this curriculum.

The sequencing has been joined with proven methods of instruction. These methods drive student understanding beyond process to deep mastery of mathematical concepts. The goal of *Eureka Math* is to produce students who are fluent, not merely literate, in mathematics.

In spite of the extensiveness of these resources, *Eureka Math* is not meant to be prescriptive. Rather, we offer it as a basis for teachers to hone their own craft. Great Minds believes deeply in the ability of teachers and in their central, irreplaceable role in shaping the classroom experience. To support and facilitate that important work, *Eureka Math* includes both scaffolding hints to help teachers support Response to Intervention (RTI) and maintains a consistent lesson structure that allows teachers to focus their energy on engaging students in the mathematical story.

In addition, the online version of *Eureka Math* (www.eureka-math.org) features embedded video that demonstrates classroom practices. The readily navigable online version includes progressions-based search functionality to permit navigation between standards and related lessons, linking all lessons in a particular standards strand or mathematical progression and learning trajectory. This functionality also helps teachers identify and remediate gaps in prerequisite knowledge, implement RTI tiers, and provide support for students at a variety of levels.

The research and development on which *Eureka Math* is based was made possible through a partnership with the New York State Education Department, for which this work was originally created. The department's expert review team, including renowned mathematicians who helped write the new standards, progressions, and the much-touted "Publishers' Criteria" (http://achievethecore.org/page/686/publishers-criteria) strengthened an already rigorous development process. We are proud to offer *Eureka Math*, an extended version of that work, to teachers all across the country.

ADVANTAGES TO A COHERENT CURRICULUM

Great Minds believes in the theory of teaching content as a coherent story from PreK to Grade 12—one that is sequential, scaffolded, and logically cohesive within and between grades. Great Minds' *Eureka Math* is a program with a three-part narrative, from A *Story of Units* (PreK–5) to A *Story of Ratios* (6–8) to A *Story of Functions* (9–12). This curriculum shows Great Minds' commitment to provide educators with the tools necessary to move students between grade levels so that their learning grows from what comes before and after.

A coherent curriculum creates a common knowledge base for all students that supports effective instruction across the classroom. Students' sharing of a base of knowledge engenders a classroom environment of common understanding and learning. This means that the effectiveness of instruction can be far more significant than when topics are taught as discrete unrelated items, as teachers can work with students to achieve a deep level of comprehension and shared learning.

This cohesiveness must be based on the foundation of a content-rich curriculum that is well organized and thoughtfully designed in order to facilitate learning at the deepest level. A coherent curriculum should be free of gaps and needless repetition, aligned to standards but also vertically and horizontally linked across lessons and grade levels. What students learn in one lesson prepares them for the next in a logical sequence. In addition, what happens in one second-grade classroom in one school closely matches what happens in another second-grade classroom, creating a shared base of understanding across students, grades, and schools.

Lack of coherence can lead to misalignment and random, disordered instruction that can prove costly to student learning and greatly increase the time that teachers spend on preparation, revisions, and repetition of material. The model of a sequential, comprehensive curriculum, such as *Eureka Math*, brings benefits within the uniformity in time spent on content, approach to instruction, and lesson structure, facilitating a common base of knowledge and an environment of shared understanding.

The commitment to uniformity influenced Great Minds' approach to creating *Eureka Math*. This curriculum was created from a single vision spanning PreK–12, with the same leadership team of mathematicians, writers, and project managers overseeing and coordinating the development of all grades at one time. By using the same project team throughout the course of *Eureka Math's* development, Great Minds was able to ensure that *Eureka Math* tells a comprehensive story with no gaps from grade to grade or band to band.

CHAPTER 2

Major Mathematical Themes in Each Grade Band

This chapter presents the year-long curriculum maps for each grade band in the *Eureka Math* curriculum: *A Story of Units*, *A Story of Ratios*, and *A Story of Functions*. These maps illustrate the major mathematical themes across the entire mathematics curriculum. The chapter also includes a detailed examination of the math concept development for *A Story of Units*, highlighting the significance of the unit. The chapter closes with an in-depth description of how the curriculum is aligned to the Instructional Shifts and the Standards for Mathematical Practice.

YEAR-LONG CURRICULUM MAPS FOR EACH GRADE BAND

The curriculum map is a chart that shows, at a glance, the sequence of modules comprising each grade of the entire curriculum for a given grade band. The map also indicates the approximate number of instructional days designated for each module of each grade. It is important for educators to have knowledge of how key topics are sequenced from PreK through Grade 12. The maps for the three grade bands in figures 2.1 to 2.3 reveal the trajectories through the grades for topics such as geometry, fractions, functions and statistics, and probability.

MATH CONTENT DEVELOPMENT FOR PREK-5: A STORY OF UNITS

The curricular design for *A Story of Units* is based on the principle that mathematics is most effectively taught as a logical, engaging story. At the elementary level, this story's main character is the basic building block of arithmetic, the unit. Themes like measurement, place value, and fractions run throughout the storyline, and each is given the amount of time proportionate to its role in the overall story. The story climaxes when students learn to add, subtract, multiply, and divide fractions; and to solve multi-step word problems with multiplicative and additive comparisons.

	PreKindergarten	Kindergarten	Grade 1	Grade 2
20 days	M1: Counting to 5 (45 days)	M1: Numbers to 10 (43 days)	M1: Sums and Differences to 10 (45 days)	M1: Sums and Differences to 20 (10 days)
				M2: Addition and Subtraction of Length Units (12 days)
20 days				M3: Place Value, Counting, and Comparison of Numbers to 1,000 (25 days)
20 days	M2: Shapes (15 days)	*M2: 2D and 3D Shapes (12 days)	M2: Introduction to Place Value Through Addition and Subtraction Within 20 (35 days)	M4: Addition and Subtraction Within 200 with Word Problems to 100 (35 days)
20 days	M3: Counting to 10 (50 days)	M3: Comparison of Length, Weight, Capacity, and Numbers to 10 (38 days)		
20 days			M3: Ordering and Comparing Length Measurements as Numbers (15 days)	M5: Addition and Subtraction Within 1,000 with Word Problems to 100 (24 days)
20 days		M4: Number Pairs, Addition and Subtraction to 10 (47 days)	M4: Place Value, Comparison, Addition and Subtraction to 40 (35 days)	M6: Foundations of Multiplication and Division (24 days)
20 days	M4: Comparison of Length, Weight, Capacity, and Numbers to 5 (35 days)		M5: Identifying, Composing, and Partitioning Shapes (15 days)	M7: Problem Solving with Length, Money, and Data (30 days)
20 days	M5: Addition and Subtraction Stories and Counting to 20 (35 days)	M5: Numbers 10–20 and Counting to 100 (30 days)	M6: Place Value, Comparison, Addition and Subtraction to 100 (35 days)	
20 days				M8: Time, Shapes, and Fractions as Equal Parts of Shapes (20 days)
		M6: Analyzing, Comparing, and Composing Shapes (10 days)		

*Please refer to grade-level descriptions to identify partially labeled modules and

Key:	Geometry	Number

Figure 2.1   Grades PreK–5 Year-Long Curriculum Map: A Story of Units

Grade 3	Grade 4	Grade 5	
M1: Properties of Multiplication and Division and Solving Problems with Units of 2–5 and 10 (25 days)	M1: Place Value, Rounding, and Algorithms for Addition and Subtraction (25 days)	M1: Place Value and Decimal Fractions (20 days)	**20 days**
M2: Place Value and Problem Solving with Units of Measure (25 days)	*M2: Unit Conversions (7 days)	M2: Multi-Digit Whole Number and Decimal Fraction Operations (35 days)	**20 days**
M3: Multiplication and Division with Units of 0, 1, 6–9, and Multiples of 10 (25 days)	M3: Multi-Digit Multiplication and Division (43 days)		**20 days**
		M3: Addition and Subtraction of Fractions (22 days)	**20 days**
M4: Multiplication and Area (20 days)	M4: Angle Measure and Plane Figures (20 days)	M4: Multiplication and Division of Fractions and Decimal Fractions (38 days)	**20 days**
M5: Fractions as Numbers on the Number Line (35 days)	M5: Fraction Equivalence, Ordering, and Operations (45 days)		**20 days**
		M5: Addition and Multiplication with Volume and Area (25 days)	**20 days**
M6: Collecting and Displaying Data (10 days)			**20 days**
M7: Geometry and Measurement Word Problems (40 days)	M6: Decimal Fractions (20 days)	M6: Problem Solving with the Coordinate Plane (40 days)	**20 days**
	M7: Exploring Measurement with Multiplication (20 days)		**20 days**

the standards corresponding to all modules.

Number and Geometry, Measurement	Fractions

	Grade 6	Grade 7	Grade 8	
20 days	M1: Ratios and Unit Rates (35 days)	M1: Ratios and Proportional Relationships (30 days)	M1: Integer Exponents and the Scientific Notation (20 days)	20 days
20 days			M2: The Concept of Congruence (25 days)	20 days
20 days	M2: Arithmetic Operations Including Division of Fractions (25 days)	M2: Rational Numbers (30 days)	M3: Similarity (25 days)	20 days
20 days	M3 Rational Numbers (25 days)	M3: Expressions and Equations (35 days)	M4: Linear Equations (40 days)	20 days
20 days	M4: Expressions and Equations (45 days)			20 days
20 days		M4: Percent and Proportional Relationships (25 days)	M5: Examples of Functions from Geometry (15 days)	20 days
20 days	M5: Area, Surface Area, and Volume Problems (25 days)	M5: Statistics and Probability (25 days)	M6: Linear Functions (20 days)	20 days
20 days		M6: Geometry (35 days)	M7: Introduction to Irrational Numbers Using Geometry (35 days)	20 days
20 days	M6: Statistics (25 days)			20 days

Key:	Number	Geometry	Ratios and Proportions	Expressions and Equations	Statistics and Probability	Functions

Figure 2.2   Grades 6–8 Year-Long Curriculum Map: A Story of Ratios

Few U.S. textbooks paint mathematics as a dynamic, unfolding tale. They instead prioritize teaching procedures and employ a spiraling approach, in which topics are partially taught and then returned to—sometimes years later—with the unrealistic expectation that students will somehow connect the dots. But teaching procedures as skills without a rich context is ineffective. Students can too easily forget procedures and will fail if they do not have deeper, more concrete knowledge from which they can draw.

THE SIGNIFICANCE OF THE UNIT

Even as new concepts are introduced to students, the overarching theme remains: defining the basic building block, the unit. Studying, relating, manipulating, and converting the unit allows students to add, subtract, complete word problems, multiply, divide, and understand concepts like place value, fractions, measurements, area, and volume. Students learn that unit-based procedures are transferable and can thus build on their knowledge in new ways. The following progressions demonstrate how the curriculum moves from the introductory structures of addition, through place value and multiplication, to operations with fractions and beyond.

	Grade 9 – Algebra I	Grade 10 – Geometry	Grade 11 – Algebra II	Grade 12 – Precalculus and Advanced Topics	
20 days	M1: Relationships Between Quantities and Reasoning with Equations and Their Graphs (40 days)	M1: Congruence, Proof, and Constructions (45 days)	M1: Polynomial, Rational, and Radical Relationships (45 days)	M1: Complex Numbers and Transformations (40 days)	20 days
20 days					20 days
20 days	M2: Descriptive Statistics (25 days)	M2: Similarity, Proof, and Trigonometry (45 days)	M2: Trigonometric Functions (20 days)	M2: Vectors and Matrices (40 days)	20 days
20 days	M3: Linear and Exponential Functions (35 days)		M3: Functions (45 days)		20 days
20 days		M3: Extending to Three Dimensions (15 days)		M3: Rational and Exponential Functions (25 days)	20 days
20 days	M4: Polynomial and Quadratic Expressions, Equations and Functions (30 days)	M4: Connecting Algebra and Geometry through Coordinates (20 days)	M4: Inferences and Conclusions from Data (40 days)	M4: Trigonometry (20 days)	20 days
20 days	M5: A Synthesis of Modeling with Equations and Functions (20 days)	M5: Circles with and Without Coordinates (25 days)		M5: Probability and Statistics (25 days)	20 days
10 days					10 days

Figure 2.3   Grades 9-12 Year-Long Curriculum Map: A Story of Functions

Numbers through 10

Initially, in PreKindergarten and Kindergarten, one object is one unit: "Let's count the frogs! The frog is one unit: 1 frog, 2 frogs, 3 frogs …" Students then relate numbers to each other and to 5 and 10. For example, in building a growth pattern (a stair-shaped structure) of unit cubes representing each number to 10 and having a color change at 5, students see that 7 is 1 unit more than 6, 1 less than 8, 2 more than 5, and 3 less than 10. That is, it can be broken into 1 and 6, or 2 and 5. Then 7 can be a unit to manipulate ("I can break it apart into 3 and 4") to be formed ("I can add 1 more to 6"), and related ("It needs 3 more to be 10").

Addition and Subtraction

In order to add 8 and 6, for example, students form a unit of 10 and add the remainder: $8 + 6 = 8 + (2 + 4) = (8 + 2) + 4 = 10 + 4 = 14$. They extend that skill by adding 18 + 6, 80 + 60, 800 kg + 600 kg, and 8 ninths + 6 ninths. This idea is easily transferable to more complex units. Adding mixed units (e.g., 2 dogs 4 puppies + 3 dogs 5 puppies) means adding like units just as in 2 tens 4 ones + 3 tens 5 ones, 2 feet 4 inches + 3 feet 5 inches, 2 hours 4 minutes + 3 hours 50 minutes, and so on.

Place Value and the Standard Algorithms

With regard to this overarching theme, the place value system is an organized, compact way to write numbers using *place value units* that are powers of 10: ones, tens, hundreds, and so on. Explanations of all standard algorithms hinge on the manipulation of these place value units and the relationships between them (e.g., 10 tens = 1 hundred).

Multiplication

One of the earliest, easiest methods of forming a new unit is by creating groups of another unit. Kindergarten students take a stick of 10 linking cubes and break it into twos. "How many cubes are in your stick?" "Ten!" "Break it and make twos." "Count your twos with me: '1 two, 2 twos, 3 twos' … We made 5 twos!" Groups of 4 apples, for example, can be counted: 1 four, 2 fours, 3 fours, 4 fours. Relating the new unit to the original unit develops the idea of multiplication: 3 groups of 4 apples equal 12 apples (or 3 fours are 12). Manipulating the new unit brings out other relationships: 3 fours + 7 fours = 10 fours or $(3 \times 4) + (7 \times 4) = (3 + 7) \times 4$.

Fractions

Forming fractional units is exactly the same as the procedure for multiplication, but the "group" can now be the amount when a whole unit is subdivided equally: A segment of length 1 can be subdivided into 4 segments of equal length, each representing the unit 1 fourth. The new unit can then be counted and manipulated just like whole numbers: 3 fourths + 7 fourths = 10 fourths.

Word Problems

Forming units to solve word problems is one of the most powerful examples of this overarching theme. Consider the following situation:

Each bottle holds 900 ml of water.
A bucket holds 6 times as much water as a bottle.
A glass holds 1/5 as much water as a bottle.

We can use the bottle capacity to form a unit pictorially and illustrate the other quantities with relationship to that unit:

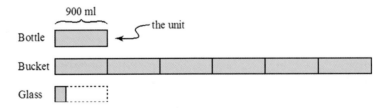

The unit can then be used to answer word problems about this situation, such as, "How much more does the bucket hold than 4 bottles?" (2 units or 1800 ml).

Once the units are established and defined, the task is simply manipulating them with arithmetic. With this repetition of prior experiences, the student realizes that he or she has seen this before.

HOW A STORY OF UNITS ALIGNS WITH THE INSTRUCTIONAL SHIFTS

A *Story of Units* is structured around the essential Instructional Shifts needed to implement the new college- and career-ready standards. These principles, articulated as three shifts (focus, coherence, and rigor), help educators understand what is required to implement the necessary changes. Rigor refers to the additional shifts of fluency, conceptual understanding, and application—and all three are done with a dual-intensity emphasis on practicing and understanding. All three Instructional Shifts are required to teach the new standards.

Shift 1: Focus—"Focus deeply on only the concepts that are prioritized in the standards."

A *Story of Units* follows the focus of the standards by relating every arithmetic idea back to understanding the idea of a unit:

- What the definition of the unit is in particular cases (e.g., whole numbers, fractions, decimals, measurements)

- Commonalities between all units (they can be added, subtracted, multiplied, and so on)

- The unique features of some units (e.g., a rectangle's area units, as opposed to its length units, can be calculated quickly by multiplying length measurements of the rectangle)

It is the study of the commonalities between units that drives the focus of A *Story of Units* so that the concepts that students learn are the ones prioritized by the standards. The commonalities form the interconnectedness of the math concepts and enable students to more easily transfer their mathematical skills and understanding across grades. Perhaps surprising, it is also the focused study of the commonalities between types of units that makes the contrast between these different types more pronounced. That is, by understanding the commonalities between types of units, students develop their ability to compare and contrast the types of units. The focus drives an understanding of the commonalities and the differences in the ways that arithmetic can be used to manipulate numbers.

Evidence of focus is seen as well in the integral use of the Partnership for Assessment of Readiness for College and Careers (PARCC) Content Emphases to focus on the major work of the grade level. Each module begins with the Focus Grade Level Standards clearly stating the clusters of standards that are emphasized in the material. As noted in the Publishers' Criteria, approximately three-quarters of the work is on the major clusters where students should be most fluent. Supporting clusters are interwoven as connecting components in core understanding while additional clusters introduce other key ideas.

Shift 2: Coherence—"Principals and teachers carefully connect the learning within and across grades so that … students can build new understanding onto foundations built in previous years."

A *Story of Units* is not a collection of topics. Rather, the modules and topics in the curriculum are woven through the progressions of the standards. A *Story of Units* carefully prioritizes and sequences those standards with a deliberate emphasis on mastery of the outlined major cluster standards. As students complete each module, this meticulous sequencing enables them to transfer their mathematical knowledge and understanding to new, increasingly challenging concepts.

Module Overview charts show how topics are aligned with standards to create an instructional sequence that is organized precisely to build on previous learning and to support future learning.

The teaching sequence chart for each topic outlines the instructional path by stating the learning objectives for each lesson. The sequence of problems in the material is structured to help teachers analyze the mathematics for themselves and help them with differentiated instruction. As students advance from simple to more complex concepts, the different problems provide opportunities for teachers to (1) break problems down for students struggling with a next step or (2) stretch problems out for those hungry for greater challenges.

Coherence is supported as well through the use of a finite set of concrete and pictorial models. As a result, students develop increasing familiarity with this limited set of consistently used models over the years. In second grade, for example, they use number disks (aka place value disks) to represent place value; that model remains constant through the third, fourth, and fifth grades. As new ideas are introduced, the consistent use of the same model leads students to more rapid and deeper understanding of new concepts.

Shift 3: Rigor—"Pursue, with equal intensity, three aspects of rigor in the major work of each grade: conceptual understanding, procedural skill and fluency, and applications."

The three-pronged nature of rigor undergirds a main theme of the Publishers' Criteria. Fluency, deep understanding, and application with equal intensity must drive instruction for students to meet the standards' rigorous expectations.

FLUENCY

"Students are expected to have speed and accuracy with simple calculations; teachers structure class time and/or homework time for students to memorize, through repetition, core functions."

Fluency represents a major part of the instructional vision that shapes A *Story of Units*; it is a daily, substantial, and sustained activity. One or two fluencies are required by the standards for each grade level, and fluency suggestions are included in most lessons. Implementation of effective fluency practice is supported by the lesson structure.

Fluency tasks are strategically designed for the teacher to easily administer and assess. A variety of suggestions for fluency activities are offered, such as mental math activities and interactive drills. Throughout the school year, such activities can be used with new material to strengthen skills and enable students to see their accuracy and speed increase measurably each day.

CONCEPTUAL UNDERSTANDING

"Students deeply understand and can operate easily within a math concept before moving on. They learn more than the trick to get the answer right. They learn the math."

Conceptual understanding requires far more than performing discrete and often disjointed procedures to determine an answer. Students must not only learn mathematical content; they must also be able to access that knowledge from numerous vantage points and communicate about the process. In A *Story of Units*, students use writing and speaking to solve mathematical problems, reflect on their learning, and analyze their thinking. Several times a week, the lessons and homework require students to write their solutions to word problems. Thus, students learn to express their understanding of concepts and articulate their thought processes through writing. Similarly, they participate in daily debriefings and learn to verbalize the patterns and connections between the current lesson and their previous learning, in addition to listening to and debating their peers' perspectives. The goal is to interweave the learning of new concepts with reflection time into students' everyday math experience.

At the module level, *sequence is everything.* Standards within a single module and modules across the year carefully build on each other to ensure that students have the requisite understanding to fully access new learning goals and integrate them into their developing schemas of understanding. The deliberate progression of the material follows the critical instructional areas outlined in the introduction of the standards for each grade.

APPLICATION

"Students are expected to use math and choose the appropriate concept for application even when they are not prompted to do so."

A *Story of Units* is designed to help students understand how to choose and apply mathematics concepts to solve problems. To achieve this, the modules include mathematical tools and diagrams that aid problem solving, interesting problems that encourage students to think quantitatively and creatively, and opportunities to model situations using mathematics. The goal is for students to see mathematics as connected to their environment, other disciplines, and the mathematics itself. Ranges of problems are presented within modules, topics, and lessons that serve multiple purposes:

- Single-step word problems that help students understand the meaning of a particular concept.

- Multistep word problems that support and develop instructional concepts and allow for cross-pollination of multiple concepts into a single problem.

- Exploratory tasks designed to break potential habits of rigid thinking. For example, asking students to draw at least three different triangles with a 15-inch perimeter encourages them to think of triangles other than equilaterals. Geometry problems with multiple solution paths and mental math problems that can be solved in many ways are further examples.

The Problem Sets are designed so that there is a healthy mix of PARCC type I, II, and III tasks:

Type I: Such tasks include computational problems, fluency exercises, conceptual problems, and applications, including one-step and multistep word problems.

Type II: These tasks require students to demonstrate reasoning skills, justify their arguments, and critique the reasoning of their peers.

Type III: For these problems, students must model real-world situations using mathematics and demonstrate more advanced problem-solving skills.

Dual intensity–"Students are practicing and understanding. There is more than a balance between these two things in the classroom–both are occurring with intensity."

A *Story of Units* achieves this goal through a balanced approach to lesson structure. Each lesson is structured to incorporate ten to twenty minutes of fluency activities, while the remaining time is devoted to developing conceptual understanding or applications–or both.

New conceptual understanding paves the way for new types of fluency. A *Story of Units* starts each grade with a variety of relevant fluency choices from the previous grade. As the year progresses and new concepts are taught, the range of choices grows. Teachers can–and are expected to–adapt their lessons to provide the intense practice with the fluencies that their students most need. Thus, A *Story of Units* doesn't wait months to spiral back to a concept. Rather, once a concept is learned, it is immediately spiraled back into the daily lesson structure through fluency and applications.

HOW A STORY OF UNITS ALIGNS WITH THE STANDARDS FOR MATHEMATICAL PRACTICE

Like the Instructional Shifts, each standard for mathematical practice is integrated into the design of A *Story of Units*.

1. **Make sense of problems and persevere in solving them.**

   An explicit way in which the curriculum integrates this standard is through its commitment to consistently engaging students in solving multistep problems. Purposeful integration of a variety of problem types that range in complexity naturally invites children to analyze givens, constraints, relationships, and goals. Problems require students to organize their thinking through drawing and modeling, which necessitates critical self-reflection on the actions they take to problem-solve. On a more foundational level, concept sequence, activities, and lesson structure present information from a variety of novel perspectives. The question, "How can I look at this differently?" undergirds the organization of the curriculum, each of its components, and the design of every problem.

2. **Reason abstractly and quantitatively.**

   The use of tape diagrams is one way in which A Story of Units provides students with opportunities to reason abstractly and quantitatively. For example, consider the following problem:

   > *A cook has a bag of rice that weighs 50 pounds. The cook buys another bag of rice that weighs 25 pounds more than the first bag. How many pounds of rice does the cook have?*

   To solve this problem, the student uses a tape diagram to abstractly represent the first bag of rice. To make a tape diagram for the second bag, the student reasons to decide whether the next bar is bigger, smaller, or the same size—and then must decide by how much. Once the student has drawn the models on paper, the fact that these quantities are presented as bags in the problem becomes irrelevant as the student shifts focus to manipulating the units to get the total. The unit has appropriately taken over the thought process necessary for solving the problem.

   Quantitative reasoning also permeates the curriculum as students focus in on units. Consider the problem "6 sevens plus 2 sevens is equal to 8 sevens." The unit being manipulated in this sequence is sevens.

3. **Construct viable arguments and critique the reasoning of others.**

   Time for debriefing is included in every daily lesson plan and represents one way in which the curriculum integrates this standard. During debriefings, teachers lead students in discussions or writing exercises that prompt children to analyze and explain their work, reflect on their own learning, and make connections between concepts. In addition to debriefings, partner sharing is woven throughout lessons to create frequent opportunities for students to develop this mathematical practice. Students use drawings, models, numeric representations, and precise language to make their learning and thinking understood by others.

4. **Model with mathematics.**

A first-grade student represents "3 students were playing. Some more came. Then there were 10. How many students came?" with the number sentence 3 + □ = 10. A fourth-grade student represents a drawing of 5 halves of apples with an expression and writes 5 × ½. Both students are modeling with mathematics. This is happening daily in word problems. Students write both "situation equations" and "solution equations" when solving word problems. In doing so, they are modeling MP.2, reason abstractly and quantitatively.

5. **Use appropriate tools strategically.**

Building students' independence with the use of models is a key feature of A Story of Units, and our approach to empowering students to use strategic learning tools is systematic. Models are introduced and used continuously so that eventually students use them automatically. The depth of familiarity that students have with the models not only ensures that they naturally become a part of students' schema but also facilitates a more rapid and deeper understanding of new concepts as they are introduced.

Aside from models, tools are introduced in Kindergarten and reappear throughout the curriculum in every concept. For example, rulers are tools that kindergartners use to create straight edges that organize their work and evenly divide their papers. They will continue to use them through Grade 5.

6. **Attend to precision.**

In every lesson of every module across the curriculum, students are manipulating, relating, and converting units and are challenged not only to use units in these ways but also to specify which unit they are using. Literally anything that can be counted can be a unit: There might be 3 frogs, 6 apples, 2 fours, 5 tens, 4 fifths, 9 cups, or 7 inches. Students use precise language to describe their work: "We used a paper clip as a unit of length." Understanding the unit is fundamental to their precise, conceptual manipulation. For example, 27 times 3 is not simply 2 times 3 and 7 times 3; rather, it should be thought of as 2 tens times 3 and 7 ones times 3. Specificity and precision with the unit is paramount to conceptual coherence and unity.

7. **Look for and make use of structure.**

There are several ways in which A Story of Units weaves this standard into the content of the curriculum. One way is through daily fluency practice. Sprints, for example, are intentionally patterned fluency activities. Students analyze the pattern of the sprint and use its discovery to assist them with automaticity—for example, "Is the pattern adding one or adding ten? How does knowing the pattern help me work faster?"

An example from a PreK lesson explicitly shows how concepts and activities are organized to guide students in identification and use of structure. In this lesson, the student is charged with the problem of using connecting cubes to make stairs for a bear to get up to his house. Students start with one cube to make the first stair. To make the second stair, students place a second cube next to the first but quickly realize that the two "stairs" are equal in height. In order to carry the bear upward, they must add another cube to the second stair so that it becomes higher than the first.

8. **Look for and express regularity in repeated reasoning.**

Mental math is one way in which A Story of Units *brings this standard to life. It begins as early as first grade, when students start to make tens. Making ten becomes both a general method and a pathway for quickly manipulating units through addition and subtraction. For example, to mentally solve 12 + 3, students identify the 1 ten and add 10 + (2 + 3). Isolating or using ten as a reference point becomes a form of repeated reasoning that allows students to quickly and efficiently manipulate units.*

In summary, the Instructional Shifts and the Standards for Mathematical Practice help establish the mechanism for thoughtful sequencing and emphasis on key topics in A Story of Units. It is evident that these pillars of the new standards combine to support the curriculum with a structural foundation for the content. Consequently, A Story of Units is artfully crafted to engage teachers and students alike while providing a powerful avenue for teaching and learning mathematics.

CHAPTER 3

Grade-Level Content Review

The Grade-Level Content Review begins with a list of modules developed to deliver instruction aligned to the standards at a given grade level. This introductory component is followed by three sections: the Summary of Year, the Rationale for Module Sequence, and the Alignment Chart with the grade-level standards. The Summary of Year portion of each grade level contains four pieces of information:

- The critical instructional areas for the grade.

- The Key Areas of Focus for the grade band.

- The Required Fluencies for the grade.

- The Major Emphasis Clusters for the grade.

The Rationale for Module Sequence portion of each grade level provides a brief description of the instructional focus of each module for that grade and explains the developmental sequence of the mathematics.

The Alignment Chart for each grade lists the standards that are addressed in each module of the grade. Throughout the alignment charts, when a cluster is included without a footnote, it is taught in its entirety; there are also times when footnotes are relevant to particular standards within a cluster. All standards for each grade have been carefully included in the module sequence. Some standards are deliberately included in more than one module, so that a strong foundation can be built over time.

The Grade-Level Content Review offers key information about grade-level content and provides a recommended framework for grouping and sequencing topics and standards.

Sequence of Grade 5 Modules Aligned with the Standards

Module 1: Place Value and Decimal Fractions

Module 2: Multi-Digit Whole Number and Decimal Fraction Operations

Module 3: Addition and Subtraction of Fractions

Module 4: Multiplication and Division of Fractions and Decimal Fractions

Module 5: Addition and Multiplication with Volume and Area

Module 6: Problem Solving with the Coordinate Plane

Summary of Year

Fifth-grade mathematics is about (1) developing fluency with addition and subtraction of fractions and developing understanding of the multiplication of fractions and division of fractions in limited cases (unit fractions divided by whole numbers and whole numbers divided by unit fractions); (2) extending division to two-digit divisors, integrating decimal fractions into the place value system and developing understanding of operations with decimals to hundredths, and developing fluency with whole number and decimal operations; and (3) developing understanding of volume.

Key Areas of Focus for Grades 3-5: Multiplication and division of whole numbers and fractions—concepts, skills, and problem solving.

Required Fluency: 5.NBT.5 Multi-digit multiplication.

Major Standard Emphasis Clusters

Number and Operations in Base Ten

- Understand the place value system.
- Perform operations with multi-digit whole numbers and with decimals to hundredths.

Number and Operations–Fractions

- Use equivalent fractions as a strategy to add and subtract fractions.
- Apply and extend previous understandings of multiplication and division to multiply and divide fractions.

Measurement and Data

- Geometric measurement: understand concepts of volume and relate volume to multiplication and to addition.

RATIONALE FOR MODULE SEQUENCE IN GRADE 5

Students' experiences with the algorithms as ways to manipulate place value units in Grades 2 to 4 really begin to pay dividends in Grade 5. In Module 1, whole number patterns with number disks on the place value table are easily generalized to decimal numbers. As students work word problems with measurements in the metric system, where the same patterns occur, they begin to appreciate the value and the meaning of decimals. They apply their work with place value to adding, subtracting, multiplying, and dividing decimal numbers with tenths and hundredths.

Module 2 begins by using place value patterns and the distributive and associative properties to multiply multi-digit numbers by multiples of 10 and leads to fluency with multi-digit whole number multiplication.[1] For multiplication, students must grapple with and fully understand the distributive property (one of the key reasons for teaching the multi-digit algorithm). Whereas the multi-digit multiplication algorithm is a straightforward generalization of the one-digit multiplication algorithm, the division algorithm with two-digit divisors requires far more care in teaching because students also have to learn estimation strategies, error correction strategies, and the idea of successive approximation (all of which are central concepts in math, science, and engineering).

Work with place value units paves the path toward fraction arithmetic in Module 3 as elementary math's place value emphasis shifts to the larger set of fractional units for algebra. Like units are added to and subtracted from like units:

$$1.5 + 0.8 = 1\frac{5}{10} + \frac{8}{10} = 15 \text{ tenths} + 8 \text{ tenths} = 23 \text{ tenths} = 2 \text{ and } 3 \text{ tenths} = 2\frac{3}{10} = 2.3$$

$$1\frac{5}{9} + \frac{8}{9} = 14 \text{ ninths} + 8 \text{ ninths} = 22 \text{ ninths} = 2 \text{ and } 4 \text{ ninths} = 2\frac{4}{9}$$

The new complexity is that when units are not equivalent, they must be changed for smaller equal units so that they can be added or subtracted. Probably the best model for showing this is the rectangular fraction model pictured below. The equivalence is then represented symbolically as students engage in active meaning making rather than obeying the perhaps mysterious command to "multiply the top and bottom by the same number":

$$2 \text{ boys} + 1 \text{ girl} = 2 \text{ children} + 1 \text{ child} = 3 \text{ children}$$

$$2 \text{ thirds} + 1 \text{ fourth} = 8 \text{ twelfths} + 3 \text{ twelfths} = 11 \text{ twelfths}$$

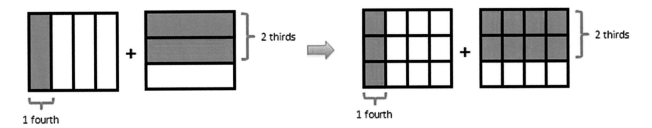

$$\frac{2}{3} + \frac{1}{4} = \left(\frac{2 \times 4}{3 \times 4}\right) + \left(\frac{1 \times 3}{4 \times 3}\right) = \frac{8}{12} + \frac{3}{12} = \frac{11}{12}$$

Relating different fractional units to one another requires extensive work with area and number line diagrams. Tape diagrams are used often in word problems. Tape diagrams, which students began using in the early grades and which become increasingly useful as students apply them to a greater variety of word problems, hit their full strength as a model when applied to fraction word problems. At the heart of a tape diagram is the now-familiar idea of forming units. In fact, forming units to solve word problems is one of the most powerful examples of the unit theme and is particularly helpful for understanding fraction arithmetic, as in the following example:

Jill had $32. She gave $\frac{1}{4}$ of her money to charity and $\frac{3}{8}$ of her money to her brother. How much did she give altogether?

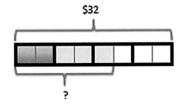

Solution with units:

8 units = $32
1 unit = $4
5 units = $20

Solution with arithmetic:

$$\frac{1}{4} + \frac{3}{8} = \frac{2}{8} + \frac{3}{8} = \frac{5}{8}$$

$$\frac{5}{8} \times 32 = 20 \qquad \text{Jill gave \$20 altogether.}$$

Near the end of Module 4, students know enough about fractions and whole number operations to begin to explore multi-digit decimal multiplication and division. In multiplying 2.1×3.8, for example, students now have multiple skills and strategies that they can use to locate the decimal point in the final answer, including:

- Unit awareness: $2.1 \times 3.8 = 21$ tenths $\times 38$ tenths $= 798$ hundredths

- Estimation (through rounding): $2.1 \times 3.8 \approx 2 \times 4 = 8$, so $2.1 \times 3.8 = 7.98$

- Fraction multiplication: $\dfrac{21}{10} \times \dfrac{38}{10} = \dfrac{(21 \times 38)}{(10 \times 10)}$

Similar strategies enrich students' understanding of division and help them to see multi-digit decimal division as whole number division in a different unit. For example, we divide to find the answer to, "How many groups of 3 apples are there in 45 apples?" and write 45 apples ÷ 3 apples = 15. Similarly, $4.5 \div 0.3$ can be written as "45 tenths ÷ 3 tenths" with the same answer: There are 15 groups of 0.3 in 4.5. This idea was used to introduce fraction division earlier in the module, thus gluing division to whole numbers, fractions, and decimals together through an understanding of units.

Frequent use of the area model in Modules 3 and 4 prepares students for an in-depth discussion of area and volume in Module 5. But the module on area and volume also reinforces work done in the fraction module: Now, questions about how the area changes when a rectangle is scaled by a whole or fractional scale factor may be asked and missing fractional sides may be found. Measuring volume once again highlights the unit theme, as a unit cube is chosen to represent a volume unit and used to measure the volume of simple shapes composed out of rectangular prisms.

Scaling is revisited in the last module on the coordinate plane. Since Kindergarten, when growth and shrinking patterns were introduced, students have been using bar graphs to display data and patterns. Extensive bar graph work has set the stage for line plots, which are both the natural extension of bar graphs and the precursor to linear functions. It is in this final module of K–5 that a simple line plot of a straight line is presented on a coordinate plane and students are asked about the scaling relationship between the increase in the units of the vertical axis for 1 unit of increase in the horizontal axis. This is the first hint of slope and marks the beginning of the major theme of middle school: ratios and proportions.

ALIGNMENT TO THE STANDARDS AND PLACEMENT OF STANDARDS IN THE MODULES

Module and Approximate Number of Instructional Days	Standards Addressed in Grade 5 Modules[2]

Module 1: Place Value and Decimal Fractions (20 days)	**Understand the place value system.**
	5.NBT.1 Recognize that in a multi-digit number, a digit in one place represents 10 times as much as it represents in the place to its right and 1/10 of what it represents in the place to its left.
	5.NBT.2 Explain patterns in the number of zeros of the product when multiplying a number by powers of 10, and explain patterns in the placement of the decimal point when a decimal is multiplied or divided by a power of 10. Use whole-number exponents to denote powers of 10.
	5.NBT.3 Read, write, and compare decimals to thousandths.
	  a. Read and write decimals to thousandths using base-ten numerals, number names, and expanded form, e.g., $347.392 = 3 \times 100 + 4 \times 10 + 7 \times 1 + 3 \times (1/10) + 9 \times (1/100) + 2 \times (1/1000)$.
	  b. Compare two decimals to thousandths based on meanings of the digits in each place, using >, =, and < symbols to record the results of comparisons.

Module and Approximate Number of Instructional Days	Standards Addressed in Grade 5 Modules[2]
	5.NBT.4 Use place value understanding to round decimals to any place. **Perform operations with multi-digit whole numbers and with decimals to hundredths.[3]** 5.NBT.7 Add, subtract, multiply, and divide decimals to hundredths, using concrete models or drawings and strategies based on place value, properties of operations, and/or the relationship between addition and subtraction; relate the strategy to a written method and explain the reasoning used. **Convert like measurement units within a given measurement system.[4]** 5.MD.1 Convert among different-sized standard measurement units within a given measurement system (e.g., convert 5 cm to 0.05 m), and use these conversions in solving multistep, real world problems.
Module 2: Multi-Digit Whole Number and Decimal Fraction Operations (35 days)	**Write and interpret numerical expressions.[5]** 5.OA.1 Use parentheses, brackets, or braces in numerical expressions, and evaluate expressions with these symbols. 5.OA.2 Write simple expressions that record calculations with numbers, and interpret numerical expressions without evaluating them. *For example, express the calculation "add 8 and 7, then multiply by 2" as 2 × (8 + 7). Recognize that 3 × (18,932 + 921) is three times as large as 18,932 + 921, without having to calculate the indicated sum or product.* **Understand the place value system.[6]** 5.NBT.1 Recognize that in a multi-digit number, a digit in one place represents 10 times as much as it represents in the place to its right and 1/10 of what it represents in the place to its left. 5.NBT.2 Explain patterns in the number of zeros of the product when multiplying a number by powers of 10, and explain patterns in the placement of the decimal point when a decimal is multiplied or divided by a power of 10. Use whole-number exponents to denote powers of 10. **Perform operations with multi-digit whole numbers and with decimals to hundredths.** 5.NBT.5 Fluently multiply multi-digit whole numbers using the standard algorithm.[7] 5.NBT.6 Find whole-number quotients of whole numbers with up to four-digit dividends and two-digit divisors, using strategies based on place value, the properties of operations, and/or the relationship between multiplication and division. Illustrate and explain the calculation by using equations, rectangular arrays, and/or area models. 5.NBT.7 Add, subtract, multiply, and divide decimals to hundredths, using concrete models or drawings and strategies based on place value, properties of operations, and/or the relationship between addition and subtraction; relate the strategy to a written method and explain the reasoning used.[8] **Convert like measurement units within a given measurement system.** 5.MD.1 Convert among different-sized standard measurement units within a given measurement system (e.g., convert 5 cm to 0.05 m), and use these conversions in solving multistep, real world problems.
Module 3: Addition and Subtraction of Fractions (22 days)	**Use equivalent fractions as a strategy to add and subtract fractions.[9]** 5.NF.1 Add and subtract fractions with unlike denominators (including mixed numbers) by replacing given fractions with equivalent fractions in such a way as to produce an equivalent sum or difference of fractions with like denominators. *For example, 2/3 + 5/4 = 8/12 + 15/12 = 23/12. (In general, a/b + c/d = (ad + bc)/bd.)* 5.NF.2 Solve word problems involving addition and subtraction of fractions referring to the same whole, including cases of unlike denominators, e.g., by using visual fraction models or equations to represent the problem. Use benchmark fractions and number sense of fractions to estimate mentally and assess the reasonableness of answers. *For example, recognize an incorrect result 2/5 + 1/2 = 3/7, by observing that 3/7 < 1/2.*
Module 4: Multiplication and Division of Fractions and Decimal Fractions (38 days)	**Write and interpret numerical expressions.** 5.OA.1 Use parentheses, brackets, or braces in numerical expressions, and evaluate expressions with these symbols. 5.OA.2 Write simple expressions that record calculations with numbers, and interpret numerical expressions without evaluating them. *For example, express the calculation "add 8 and 7, then multiply by 2" as 2 × (8 + 7). Recognize that 3 × (18,932 + 921) is three times as large as 18,932 + 921, without having to calculate the indicated sum or product.*

(Continued)

Module and Approximate Number of Instructional Days	Standards Addressed in Grade 5 Modules[2]

Perform operations with multi-digit whole numbers and with decimals to hundredths.[10]

5.NBT.7 Add, subtract, multiply, and divide decimals to hundredths, using concrete models or drawings and strategies based on place value, properties of operations, and/or the relationship between addition and subtraction; relate the strategy to a written method and explain the reasoning used.

Apply and extend previous understandings of multiplication and division to multiply and divide fractions.[11]

5.NF.3 Interpret a fraction as division of the numerator by the denominator $(a/b = a \div b)$. Solve word problems involving division of whole numbers leading to answers in the form of fractions or mixed numbers, e.g., by using visual fraction models or equations to represent the problem. *For example, interpret 3/4 as the result of dividing 3 by 4, noting that 3/4 multiplied by 4 equals 3, and that when 3 wholes are shared equally among 4 people each person has a share of size 3/4. If 9 people want to share a 50-pound sack of rice equally by weight, how many pounds of rice should each person get? Between what two whole numbers does your answer lie?*

5.NF.4 Apply and extend previous understandings of multiplication to multiply a fraction or whole number by a fraction.

  a. Interpret the product $(a/b) \times q$ as a parts (a/b) in the formula of a partition of q into b equal parts; equivalently, as the result of a sequence of operations $a \times q \div b$. *For example, use a visual fraction model to show (2/3) × 4 = 8/3, and create a story context for this equation. Do the same with (2/3) × (4/5) = 8/15. (In general, (a/b) × (c/d) = ac/bd.)*

5.NF.5 Interpret multiplication as scaling (resizing), by:

  a. Comparing the size of a product to the size of one factor on the basis of the size of the other factor, without performing the indicated multiplication.

  b. Explaining why multiplying a given number by a fraction greater than 1 results in a product greater than the given number (recognizing multiplication by whole numbers greater than 1 as a familiar case); explaining why multiplying a given number by a fraction less than 1 results in a product smaller than the given number; and relating the principle of fraction equivalence $a/b = (n \times a)/(n \times b)$ to the effect of multiplying a/b by 1.

5.NF.6 Solve real world problems involving multiplication of fractions and mixed numbers, e.g., by using visual fraction models or equations to represent the problem.

5.NF.7 Apply and extend previous understandings of division to divide unit fractions by whole numbers and whole numbers by unit fractions. (Students able to multiply fractions in general can develop strategies to divide fractions in general, by reasoning about the relationship between multiplication and division. But division of a fraction by a fraction is not a requirement at this grade.)

  a. Interpret division of a unit fraction by a non-zero whole number, and compute such quotients. *For example, create a story context for (1/3) ÷ 4, and use a visual fraction model to show the quotient. Use the relationship between multiplication and division to explain that (1/3) ÷ 4 = 1/12 because (1/12) × 4 = 1/3.*

  b. Interpret division of a whole number by a unit fraction, and compute such quotients. *For example, create a story context for 4 ÷ (1/5), and use a visual fraction model to show the quotient. Use the relationship between multiplication and division to explain that 4 ÷ (1/5) = 20 because 20 × (1/5) = 4.*

  c. Solve real world problems involving division of unit fractions by non-zero whole numbers and division of whole numbers by unit fractions, e.g., by using visual fraction models and equations to represent the problem. *For example, how much chocolate will each person get if 3 people share 1/2 lb of chocolate equally? How many 1/3-cup servings are in 2 cups of raisins?*

Module and Approximate Number of Instructional Days	Standards Addressed in Grade 5 Modules[2]
	Convert like measurement units within a given measurement system.[12]
	5.MD.1 Convert among different-sized standard measurement units within a given measurement system (e.g., convert 5 cm to 0.05 m), and use these conversions in solving multistep, real world problems.
	Represent and interpret data.
	5.MD.2 Make a line plot to display a data set of measurements in fractions of a unit (1/2, 1/4, 1/8). Use operations on fractions for this grade to solve problems involving information presented in line plots. *For example, given different measurements of liquid in identical beakers, find the amount of liquid each beaker would contain if the total amount in all the beakers were redistributed equally.*
Module 5: Addition and Multiplication with Volume and Area (25 days)	**Apply and extend previous understandings of multiplication and division to multiply and divide fractions.**[13]
	5.NF.4 Apply and extend previous understandings of multiplication to multiply a fraction or whole number by a fraction.
	b. Find the area of a rectangle with fractional side lengths by tiling it with unit squares of the appropriate unit fraction side lengths, and show that the area is the same as would be found by multiplying the side lengths. Multiply fractional side lengths to find areas of rectangles, and represent fraction products as rectangular areas.
	5.NF.6 Solve real world problems involving multiplication of fractions and mixed numbers, e.g., by using visual fraction models or equations to represent the problem.
	Geometric measurement: understand concepts of volume and relate volume to multiplication and to addition.
	5.MD.3 Recognize volume as an attribute of solid figures and understand concepts of volume measurement.
	a. A cube with side length 1 unit, called a "unit cube," is said to have "one cubic unit" of volume, and can be used to measure volume.
	b. A solid figure which can be packed without gaps or overlaps using n unit cubes is said to have a volume of n cubic units.
	5.MD.4 Measure volumes by counting unit cubes, using cubic cm, cubic in, cubic ft, and improvised units.
	5.MD.5 Relate volume to the operations of multiplication and addition and solve real world and mathematical problems involving volume.
	a. Find the volume of a right rectangular prism with whole-number side lengths by packing it with unit cubes, and show that the volume is the same as would be found by multiplying the edge lengths, equivalently by multiplying the height by the area of the base. Represent threefold whole-number products as volumes, e.g., to represent the associative property of multiplication.
	b. Apply the formulas $V = l \times w \times h$ and $V = b \times h$ for rectangular prisms to find volumes of right rectangular prisms with whole-number edge lengths in the context of solving real world and mathematical problems.
	c. Recognize volume as additive. Find volumes of solid figures composed of two non-overlapping right rectangular prisms by adding the volumes of the non-overlapping parts, applying this technique to solve real world problems.
	Classify two-dimensional figures into categories based on their properties.
	5.G.3 Understand that attributes belonging to a category of two-dimensional figures also belong to all subcategories of that category. *For example, all rectangles have four right angles and squares are rectangles, so all squares have four right angles.*
	5.G.4 Classify two-dimensional figures in a hierarchy based on properties.

(Continued)

Module and Approximate Number of Instructional Days	Standards Addressed in Grade 5 Modules[2]
Module 6: Problem Solving with the Coordinate Plane (40 days)	**Write and interpret numerical expressions.** 5.OA.2 Write simple expressions that record calculations with numbers and interpret numerical expressions without evaluating them. *For example, express the calculation "add 8 and 7, then multiply by 2" as 2 × (8 + 7). Recognize that 3 × (18,932 + 921) is three times as large as 18,932 + 921, without having to calculate the indicated sum or product.* **Analyze patterns and relationships.** 5.OA.3 Generate two numerical patterns using two given rules. Identify apparent relationships between corresponding terms. Form ordered pairs consisting of corresponding terms from the two patterns, and graph the ordered pairs on a coordinate plane. *For example, given the rule "Add 3" and the starting number 0, and given the rule "Add 6" and the starting number 0, generate terms in the resulting sequences, and observe that the terms in one sequence are twice the corresponding terms in the other sequence. Explain informally why this is so.* **Graph points on the coordinate plane to solve real world and mathematical problems.** 5.G.1 Use a pair of perpendicular number lines, called axes, to define a coordinate system, with the intersection of the lines (the origin) arranged to coincide with the 0 on each line and a given point in the plane located by using an ordered pair of numbers, called its coordinates. Understand that the first number indicates how far to travel from the origin in the direction of one axis, and the second number indicates how far to travel in the direction of the second axis, with the convention that the names of the two axes and the coordinates correspond (e.g., *x*-axis and *x*-coordinate, *y*-axis and *y*-coordinate). 5.G.2 Represent real world and mathematical problems by graphing points in the first quadrant of the coordinate plane, and interpret coordinate values of points in the context of the situation.

CHAPTER 4

Curriculum Design

Curriculum design details the approach to modules, lessons, and assessment in A *Story of Units*. This chapter describes the key elements in the modules, as well as the role each plays in successful implementation of the new standards. We provide a wealth of information about how to achieve the components of instructional rigor (fluency, concept development, and application) that the standards demand.

APPROACH TO MODULE STRUCTURE

One of the first steps in designing a curriculum to implement the standards is to determine the grouping and sequencing of the standards at each grade level. This process should be well thought out, and decisions should be based on sound rationale. It is imperative that standards for a particular grade level be structured appropriately and addressed adequately.

Making key information available to classroom teachers in each module or unit of study helps to ensure successful implementation of the standards. The authors of the curriculum included numerous features to assist teachers not only in their day-to-day classroom activities but also in developing their understanding of the mathematics content and the standards.

Each module has four primary parts: Module Overview, Topic Overviews, Lessons, and Assessments:

- The Module Overview, rich with valuable information, introduces the key components of each module. It outlines the progression of the lessons from the beginning of the module to the end. The components of the overview are as follows:
  - The opening narrative explains the progression of the mathematics through the module topic by topic.
  - Distribution of Instructional Minutes is a diagram that suggests a possible distribution of class time based on the emphasis of particular lesson components in different lessons throughout the module.
  - Focus Grade-Level Standards are the major standards that the module targets.

- ○ Foundational Standards are prerequisite knowledge that support the Focus Grade-Level Standards. These include standards addressed prior to the module that are essential for student learning and understanding. This section can be helpful in preparing for teaching lessons and for addressing any gaps that might crop up, especially during the first couple of years of implementation.
- ○ Focus Standards for Mathematical Practice act as a guide to create a well-rounded, standards-aligned classroom environment. This module element highlights which of the eight Standards for Mathematical Practice are a focus of the module and explains how each is addressed in the module.
- ○ Overview of Module Topics and Lesson Objectives lists each topic in the module, along with the associated standards and lesson objectives. The chart provides the number of days allotted for coverage of each topic. The chart also notes when the Mid-Module and End-of-Module Assessments should be administered during the module and how much time is allotted for each.
- ○ Terminology consists of both new and recently introduced terms and familiar terms and symbols. Descriptions, examples, and illustrations of the terms are included in this section.
- ○ Suggested Tools and Representations provides teachers with a list of the models, manipulatives, diagrams, and so forth that are recommended to teach the content of the module.
- ○ The Assessment Summary gives key information about the assessments of the module, including where within the module they are given and what standards are addressed.

- The Topic Overview lists the Focus Standards associated with the topic. It also provides a narrative similar to that found in the Module Overview but with information regarding specific lessons within the topic. The overview also offers Coherence Links, which reference other modules in the curriculum giving teachers access to foundational and more advanced material related to the topic. A chart detailing the objectives for each lesson is the final feature of the overview.

- Lessons and Assessments are the remaining primary parts of the module. The sections that follow detail these module components.

APPROACH TO LESSON STRUCTURE

Fluency, concept development, and application, all components of instructional rigor, are demanded by the new standards (see Instructional Shifts in chapter 2) and should be layered into daily lessons to help guide students through the mathematics. Lessons must be structured to incorporate fluency activities along with the development of conceptual understanding, procedural skills, and problem solving. Ideally, these components are taught through the deliberate progression of material from concrete to pictorial to abstract. All stages of instruction ought to be designed to help students reach higher and higher levels of understanding. The lesson design in A Story of Units reflects these ideals and is an exemplary model of how to achieve the demands the standards necessitates.

Through a balanced approach to lesson design, A Story of Units supports the development of an increasingly complex understanding of the mathematical concepts and topics within the standards. This type of balanced approach to lesson design naturally surfaces patterns and connections between concepts, tools, strategies, and real-world applications. Each lesson has a distinct structure made up of four primary components.

The time spent on each component in a daily lesson should vary between lessons and is guided by the rigor emphasized in the standard the lesson is addressing (figures 4.1 and 4.2). For example, if the word *fluently* is used within the text of a standard, a lesson involving that standard will often have more time devoted to Fluency Practice and Concept Development than to Application Problem. If the word *understand* is used in the text of a standard, then Concept Development is more likely to be weighted heavily. In the same way, the phrase *real-world problems* in the text of a standard will lead to a lesson that concentrates more on application problems. The Student Debrief component concludes the lesson with yet another carefully orchestrated opportunity for students to engage in one or more mathematical practice standards. It also provides time for reflection and consolidation of understanding.

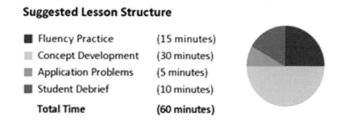

Suggested Lesson Structure

■ Fluency Practice	(15 minutes)
▫ Concept Development	(30 minutes)
▪ Application Problems	(5 minutes)
■ Student Debrief	(10 minutes)
Total Time	**(60 minutes)**

Figure 4.1   Suggested Lesson Structure

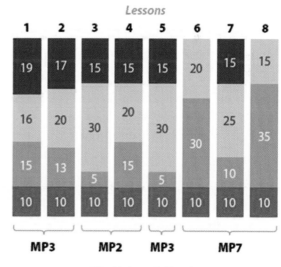

Distribution of Instructional Minutes

This diagram represents a suggested distribution of instructional minutes based on the emphasis of particular lesson components in different lessons throughout the module.

■ **Fluency Practice**
▫ **Concept Lesson**
▪ **Application Problems**
■ **Student Debrief**

MP = Mathematical Practice

Figure 4.2   Distribution of Instructional Minutes

The time devoted to each of the four components of a lesson can be viewed at a glance using the Distribution of Instructional Minutes chart from the Module Overview. The actual order of Fluency Practice, Application Problem, Concept Development, and Student Debrief in each lesson is determined by the objective. In general, however, fluency is first because animated, adrenaline-rich work gets students ready to learn for the Application Problem and Concept Development. Solving a word problem before the Concept Development serves a variety of purposes, for example, giving a new concept a meaningful context or reviewing important understandings necessary for the new concept. The Student Debrief wraps up the ideas learned for the day and is the metacognitive component of the lesson structure (see its description later in this chapter).

The lesson structure we have just set out, consisting of four major components, is not the way to meet the demands for quality instruction. There are good reasons to change the structure at times. We use this suggested lesson structure for the most part but do at times reposition or omit a component, for example, positioning the Application Problem to follow the Concept Development, omitting it entirely, or omitting the fluency for a day. More significant reorganizations do occur during explorations. The Instructional Shifts require that the three components of rigor be taught with equal intensity. Although this does not mean an equal amount of time for each component every day, any alternative lesson structure needs to meet the high expectations demanded by the standards for all three components of rigor in the major work of each grade.

FLUENCY PRACTICE

Fluency is designed to promote automaticity by engaging students in practice in ways that excite and intrigue them as well as get their adrenaline flowing. Automaticity is critical so that students avoid using up too many of their attention resources with lower-level skills when they are addressing higher-level problems. Automaticity prepares students with the computational foundation to enable deep understanding in flexible ways.

We suggest that for the first three weeks of school, teachers include *at minimum* 10 minutes of daily fluency work. This is generally high-paced and energetic work, celebrating improvement and focusing on recognizing patterns and connections within the material. Early in the year, we want students to see their skills grow significantly on both the individual and class levels. Like opening a basketball practice with team drills and exercises, both personal and group improvements are exciting and prepare the players for application in the game setting.

A *Story of Units* offers fluency activities that teachers may either select and use or study and then create their own. Fluency activities for each lesson are intentionally organized so that activities revisit previously learned material to develop automaticity, anticipate future concepts, and strategically preview or build skills for the day's concept development. It is important to provide ample opportunities to review familiar fluencies as needed, as well as to begin developing automaticity with new ones. The suggestions may or may not be ideal for the students in a given class. As teachers work with the materials, they should adjust them to fit their students' needs.

Like drills in sports, the value of structured fluency practice should be immediately recognizable to students. Becoming proficient and staying proficient at math can be compared to doing the same in sports: use it or lose it.

CONCEPT DEVELOPMENT

Intentional sequencing of standards and topics across a grade ensures that students have the requisite understanding to fully access new learning goals and integrate them into their developing schemas. The conceptual development portion of a lesson articulates the standards and topics through a deliberate progression of material, from concrete to pictorial to abstract. This structure complements and supports an increasingly complex understanding of concepts.

Of course, not every lesson can move in this exact order. Sometimes the concrete level has been covered in a prior grade level. Sometimes the lesson moves from the abstract to the pictorial or concrete. For example, in "Draw a picture of 4 + 4 + 4," and "With your number disks [or bundles], show me 248 + 100," students begin with the abstract number problem and illustrate the idea pictorially or concretely.

The goal is always to strengthen students' understanding of numbers rather than to teach manipulatives. The concrete is important when conceptual understanding is weak. Manipulatives are expensive in terms of instructional minutes. However, omitting them can sometimes result in elongating the learning process if students have failed to miss a critical connection. When necessary, it is better to take the time to reestablish meaning at the concrete and pictorial levels and move as efficiently as possible to the abstract.

In A *Story of Units*, Concept Development constitutes the major portion of instruction and generally comprises at least twenty minutes of the total lesson time. It is the primary lesson component in which new learning is introduced. Concept Development elaborates on the "how-to" of delivery through models, sample vignettes, and dialogue, all meant to give teachers a snapshot of what the classroom might look and sound like at each step of the way. Teachers' word choices may be different from those in the vignettes, and they should use what works from the suggested talking points, along with their knowledge of their students' needs, as they write their own.

APPLICATION PROBLEMS

A *Story of Units* models a design that helps students understand how to choose and apply the correct mathematics concept to solve real-world problems. To achieve this, lessons use tools and models, problems that cause students to think quantitatively and creatively, and patterns that repeat so frequently that students come to see them as connected to their environment and other disciplines.

There are clearly different possible choices for delivery of instruction when engaging in problem solving. The beginning of the year should be characterized by establishing routines that encourage hard, intelligent work through guided practice rather than exploration. This practice serves to model the behaviors that students will need to work independently later. It is also wise to clearly establish a very different tone of work on application problems from that of the "quick answers" of fluency—for example, "We just did some fast math. Now let's slow down and take more time with these problems."

The more students participate in reasoning through problems with a systematic approach, the more they internalize those behaviors and thought processes. In A *Story of Units*, lessons provide application problems that directly relate to Concept Development. Students are encouraged to solve these problems using the following steps of read-draw-write (RDW):

1. **Read the problem.**

2. **Draw and label.**

3. **Write a number sentence and a word sentence.**

While moving through the RDW process, students ask themselves questions: *What do I see? Can I draw something? What conclusions can I make from my drawing?*

STUDENT DEBRIEF

In A *Story of Units*, the Student Debrief closes the lesson, but generally lessons should allow time for reflection and consolidation of understanding. This component in the *Eureka Math* curriculum models how a teacher might approach lesson closure.

Rather than stating the objective of the lesson to the students at its beginning, we wait until the dynamic action of the lesson has taken place. Then we reflect back on it with the students to analyze the learning that occurred. We want *them* to articulate the focus of the lesson. In the Student Debrief, we develop students' metacognition by helping them make connections between parts of the lesson, concepts, strategies, and tools on their own. We draw out or introduce key vocabulary by helping students appropriately name the learning they describe.

The goal is for students to see and hear multiple perspectives from their classmates and mentally construct a multifaceted image of the concepts they are learning. Through questions that help make these connections explicit and dialogue that directly engages students in the Standards for Mathematical Practice, they articulate those observations so that the lesson's objective becomes clear to them.

Like the other lesson components, the Student Debrief includes suggested lists of questions to invite the reflection and active processing of the totality of the lesson. The purpose of these talking points is to guide teachers' planning for eliciting higher-order thinking by students. Rather than ask all of the questions provided, teachers should use those that resonate most as they consider what will best support students in articulating the focus from the lesson's multiple perspectives.

Sharing and analyzing high-quality student work is a consistent feature of the vignettes in this section. This technique encourages students to engage in the mathematical practices, which they come to value and respect as much as or more than speed in calculation. What the teacher values, the students will too; sharing and analyzing high-quality work gives teachers the opportunity to model and then demand authentic student work and dialogue.

Conversation constitutes a primary medium through which learning occurs in the Student Debrief. Teachers can prepare students by establishing routines for talking early in the year. For example, pair sharing is an invaluable structure to build for this and other components of the lesson. During the debrief, teachers should circulate as students share, noting which partnerships are bearing fruit and which need support. They might join struggling communicators for a moment to give them sentence stems. Regardless of the scaffolding techniques that a teacher decides to use, all students should be clear enough on the lesson's focus to either give a good example or make a statement about it.

Exit Tickets close the Student Debrief component of each lesson. These short, formative assessments are meant to provide quick glimpses of the day's major learning for students and teacher. Through this routine, students grow accustomed to showing accountability for each day's learning and produce valuable data for the teacher that become an indispensable planning tool.

STANDARDS FOR MATHEMATICAL PRACTICE

The Standards for Mathematical Practice are seamlessly woven into each lesson through various components of delivery that require the level of thinking and behaviors that the practices embody. The following examples from A *Story of Units* illustrate how teachers might integrate mathematical practices into daily lessons:

- Carefully crafted fluency activities engage students in looking for and making use of structure, as well as looking for and expressing regularity in repeated reasoning.

- The RDW sequence on which problem solving is based provides opportunities for students to select appropriate tools, model word problems using mathematics, and reason abstractly and quantitatively.

- Concept Development consistently invites students to make sense of problems and persevere in solving them as they grapple with new learning through increasingly complex concrete, pictorial, and abstract applications.

- Each lesson's Student Debrief, as well as ongoing debriefing embedded within each lesson component, requires students to construct arguments and critique the reasoning of others. Questioning and dialogue throughout the lessons ensure that students are not only engaging in the standards, but also that they are explicitly aware of, and reflecting on, those behaviors.

SAMPLE LESSON

In order to clearly illustrate the approach to lesson structure described above, a sample lesson follows. This is Lesson 3 from Grade 5 Module 5 whose objective is to compose and decompose right rectangular prisms using layers. Although Concept Development often follows Fluency Practice, this lesson provides an example of another lesson component, Application Problem, as the second component of the lesson.

Lesson 3

Objective: Compose and decompose right rectangular prisms using layers.

Suggested Lesson Structure

■ Fluency Practice   (12 minutes)
▨ Application Problem   (6 minutes)
□ Concept Development   (32 minutes)
■ Student Debrief   (10 minutes)
  Total Time   **(60 minutes)**

Fluency Practice (12 minutes)

- Sprint: Multiply a Fraction and a Whole Number **5.NF.3**   (8 minutes)
- Find the Volume **5.MD.3**   (4 minutes)

Sprint: Multiply a Fraction and Whole Number (8 minutes)

Materials: (S) Multiply a Fraction and Whole Number Sprint

Note: This Sprint reviews content from G5–M4–Lessons 6–8.

Figure 4.3

Find the Volume (4 minutes)

Materials: (S) Personal white boards

Note: This fluency reviews G5–M5–Lessons 1–2.

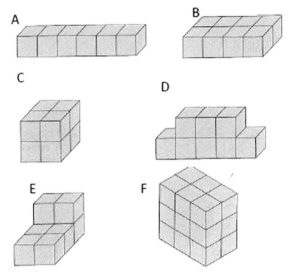

T: (Project Image A, pictured at right.) Each cube is 1 cubic centimeter. Respond on your board. How many cubes are there?

S: 6.

T: Write the volume on your board with the correct units.

S: 6 cubic centimeters.

Follow this sequence for the other images pictured to the right.

Application Problem (6 minutes)

An ice cube tray has two rows of 8 cubes in each. How many ice cubes are in a stack of 12 ice cube trays? Draw a picture to explain your reasoning.

Note: This problem encourages students to visualize layers in the stack that will be helpful as students refine their understanding of volume in today's lesson.

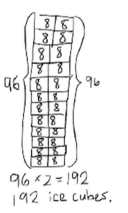

Concept Development (32 minutes)

Materials: (T) 20 centimeter cubes (S) 20 centimeter cubes, rectangular prism recording sheet

T: Build this with your own cubes. (Show 4 cubes in a square formation stacked vertically—2 layers with 2 cubes in each layer.)

T: What's the volume of this rectangular prism?

S: 4 cubic centimeters.

T: Let's add layers horizontally. Add another layer *next* to the first one.

S: (Work.)

T: What is the volume?

S: 8 cubic centimeters.

T: Add 3 more layers next to the first two. (Pause for students to do this.)

T: What is the volume now?

S: 20 cubic centimeters.

T: How did you figure that out? Turn and talk.

S: I added the first 8 to the 12 more that I added. I saw 5 along the bottom, and there were 2 layers going back, so that makes 10, and 2 layers going up makes 20. I knew that I had 20 cubes to start, and I used them all up.

Figure 4.3   (Continued)

T: (Project a blank rectangular prism from the recording sheet or draw one on the board.) Let's record how we built the layers. Use the first rectangle in the row of your recording sheet.

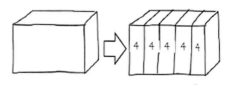

$$4\ cm^3 + 4\ cm^3 + 4\ cm^3 + 4\ cm^3 + 4\ cm^3 = 20\ cubic\ cm$$
$$5 \times 4\ cubic\ cm = 20\ cm3$$

T: How many layers did we build in all?

S: 5.

T: Let's show that by partitioning the prism into 5 layers. (Partition the prism vertically into 5 equal sections.) Make your prism look like mine. How many cubes were in each layer?

S: 4 cubes.

T: Record that on each layer that we drew. (Write a 4 on each of the horizontal layers.) Write a number sentence that expresses the volume of this prism using these layers. Turn and talk.

S: We could write 4 cubic cm + 4 cubic cm + 4 cubic cm + 4 cubic cm + 4 cubic cm = 20 cubic cm. → Since all the layers are the same, we could write 5 × 4 cubic cm = 20 cubic cm.

T: (Draw the table on the board.) I'll record that in a table. Now, imagine that we could partition this prism into layers like a cake, like our ice cube trays. What might that look like? Work with your partner to show the layers on the next prism in the row and tell how many cubes would be in each. Use your cubes to help you.

Number of Layers	Cubes in Each Layer	Volume
5	4	20 cm³
2	10	20 cm³
2	10	20 cm³

MP.4

S: The prism is 2 units high, so we could cut the prism in half horizontally from left to right. That would be 10 cubes in each one. We could make a top layer of 10 cubes and a bottom layer of 10 cubes.

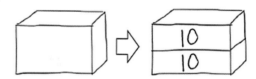

$$10\ cm^3 + 10\ cm^3 = 20\ cm^3$$
$$2 \times 10\ cubic\ cm = 20\ cubic\ cm$$

T: Let's record your thinking. (Draw the figure to the right.) Write a number sentence that expresses the volume of the prism using these layers.

S: 10 cubic cm + 10 cubic cm = 20 cubic cm 2 cubic cm × 10 cubic cm = 20 cubic cm.

T: Let's record that information in our table. (Record.) Work with your partner to find one last way that we can partition this prism into layers. Label the layers with the number of cubes on the third prism in the row, and write a number sentence to explain your thinking.

S: (Work to draw the third figure and write the number sentences.)

T: I'll record this last bit of information in our table. (Record.)

T: Now, let's draw the different layers together. Use the last prism in the row of your recording sheet.

Step 1: Draw vertical lines to show the 5 layers of 4 cubes each that remind us of bread slices. (Point to table's first line.)

Step 2: Draw a horizontal line to show the two layers of 10 cubes each that remind us of layers of cake. (Point to table's second line.)

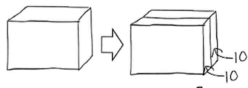

$$10\ cm^3 + 10\ cm^3 = 20\ cm^3$$
$$2 \times 10\ cubic\ cm = 20\ cubic\ cm.$$

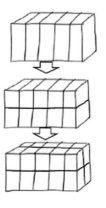

Figure 4.3 (Continued)

Step 3: Draw both a horizontal and a vertical line to show the 2 front and back layers of 10 each. (Point to table's last line.)

T: What is the volume of the cube?

S: 20 cubic centimeters.

T: Build a prism with a partner that has one 3 cube by 3 cube layer. (Demonstrate building this with cubes.)

T: What is the volume?

S: 9 cubic centimeters.

T: Add another layer of cubes on top.

T: What is the volume now? How do you know?

S: It's 18 cubic centimeters, because now we have 2 groups of 9 cubic centimeters. Two layers with 9 cubes each is 18 cubic centimeters.

T: Now add another layer. What is the volume?

S: 27 cubic centimeters.

T: What is the overall shape of your rectangular prism?

S: A cube!

T: Use the set of cubes on your recording sheet to show the three ways of layering using the same system we just did with our 2 by 2 by 5 rectangular prism.

S: (Work.)

T: (Project or draw an image of a 3 × 4 × 5 rectangular prism. Direct students to the set of vertical prisms on the prism recording sheet.) Imagine what the bottom layer of this prism would look like. Describe it to your partner and then build it.

S: There would be 3 rows with 4 cubes in each row. There would be 12 cubes in all. It would be 3 cubes wide and 4 cubes long and 1 cube high. This would be like a 4 by 3 rectangle, but it is 1 centimeter tall. (Build.)

T: Here's the same prism, but without the unit cubes drawn. How might we represent the bottom layer on this picture? Use your recording sheet, and talk to your partner.

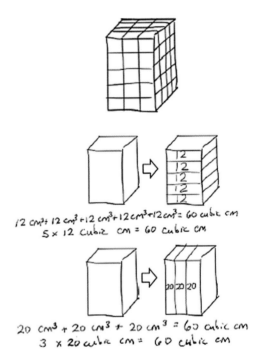

$12\ cm^3 + 12\ cm^3 + 12\ cm^3 + 12\ cm^3 + 12\ cm^3 = 60$ cubic cm

5×12 cubic cm = 60 cubic cm

$20\ cm^3 + 20\ cm^3 + 20\ cm^3 = 60$ cubic cm

3×20 cubic cm = 60 cubic cm

Figure 4.3 (Continued)

S: We could draw a horizontal slice toward the bottom and label it with 12. I can see in the drawing that there are 5 layers in all, so I'll need to make the bottom about 1 fifth of the prism and put 12 on it.

T: What is the volume of the single layer?

S: 12 cubic centimeters.

T: What is the volume of the prism with 5 of these layers?

S: It's 12 × 5, so 60. I know there are 5 layers that are the same, so 12 + 12 + 12 + 12 + 12, so 60.

T: What other ways could we partition this prism into layers? Turn and talk, then draw a picture of your thinking on the recording sheet.

S: (Draw.)

$$15 \text{ cm}^3 + 15 \text{cm}^3 + 15 \text{ cm}^3 + 15 \text{ cm}^3 = 60 \text{ cubic cm}$$
$$4 \times 15 \text{ cubic cm} = 60 \text{ cubic cm}$$

Problem Set (10 minutes)

Students should do their personal best to complete the Problem Set within the allotted 10 minutes. For some classes, it may be appropriate to modify the assignment by specifying which problems they work on first. Some problems do not specify a method for solving. Students solve these problems using the RDW approach used for Application Problems.

Student Debrief (10 minutes)

Lesson Objective: Compose and decompose right rectangular prisms using layers.

The Student Debrief is intended to invite reflection and active processing of the total lesson experience.

Invite students to review their solutions for the Problem Set. They should check work by comparing answers with a partner before going over answers as a class. Look for misconceptions or misunderstandings that can be addressed in the Debrief. Guide students in a conversation to debrief the Problem Set and process the lesson.

You may choose to use any combination of the questions below to lead the discussion.

- In Problem 1, how did you decide how to go about decomposing the prisms? Is there a different way or order in which you could have done it?

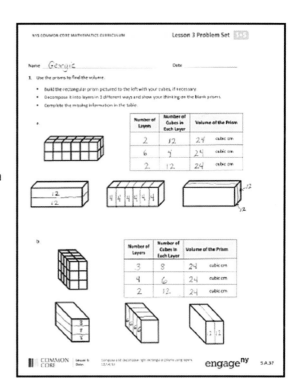

Figure 4.3 (Continued)

- Problem 4 uses meters instead of centimeters. What, if anything, did that change in how you drew your picture? How about in how you figured out the volume?

- Which layers are easier for you to visualize? Which are the hardest? What do you think about to make the hardest layers easier to see? What was Josh having a hard time visualizing in Problem 2?

- At what point did you not need to model with the physical cubes anymore?

- How did the Application Problem connect to today's lesson? How are stacks of ice trays different from the prisms in the lesson?

Exit Ticket (3 minutes)

After the Student Debrief, instruct students to complete the Exit Ticket. A review of their work will help you assess the students' understanding of the concepts that were presented in the lesson today and plan more effectively for future lessons. You may read the questions aloud to the students.

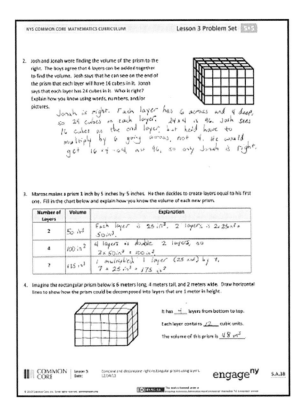

Figure 4.3 (Continued)

APPROACH TO ASSESSMENT

Assessments provide an opportunity for students to show their learning accomplishments in addition to offering them a pathway to monitor their progress, celebrate successes, examine mistakes, uncover misconceptions, and engage in self-reflection and analysis. A central goal of the assessment system as a whole is to make students aware of their strengths and weaknesses and to give them opportunities to try again, do better, and, in doing so, enjoy the experience of seeing their intelligent, hard work pay off as their skill and understanding increase. Furthermore, the data collected as a result of the assessments represent an invaluable tool in the hands of teachers and provide them with specific data about student understanding to direct their instruction.

In *A Story of Units*, assessment becomes a regular part of the class routine in the form of daily, mid-module, and end-of-module appraisal. Both the mid-module tasks and the end-of-module tasks are designed to allow quick scoring that make it possible for teachers to implement instructionally relevant, actionable feedback to students and to monitor student progress to determine the effectiveness of their instruction and make any needed adjustments. These mid-module and end-of-module tasks should be used in combination with instructionally embedded tasks, teacher-developed quizzes, and other formative assessment strategies in order to realize the full benefits of data-driven instruction.

DAILY FORMATIVE ASSESSMENTS

Problem Sets

As part of Concept Development, students may be asked to work on a Problem Set, either independently or with teacher guidance. They can be checked in class as part of the lesson. The Problem Sets often include fluency pertaining to the Concept Development, as well as conceptual and application word problems. The primary goal of the Problem Set is for students to apply the conceptual understandings learned during the lesson. Students work intently for a specified period of time, but the number of problems completed during this time will vary from student to student.

Exit Tickets

Exit Tickets are a critical element of the lesson structure. These quick assessments contain specific questions about what students learned that day. The purpose of the Exit Ticket is twofold: to teach students to grow accustomed to being held individually accountable for the work they have done after one day's instruction and to provide the teacher with valuable evidence of the efficacy of that day's work—which is indispensable for planning purposes.

Homework

Similar in content and format to the Problem Sets, Homework gives students additional practice on the skills they learn in class each day. The idea is not to introduce brand-new concepts or ideas, but to build student confidence with the material learned in class. Having already worked similar problems in class, the Homework gives students a chance to check their understanding and confirm that they can do the problems independently.

MID-MODULE ASSESSMENT TASK

A Mid-Module Assessment Task is provided for each module, specifically tailored to address approximately the first half of the learning objectives for which the module is designed. Careful articulation in a rubric provides guidance in understanding common preconceptions or misconceptions of students for discrete portions of knowledge or skill on their way to proficiency for each standard and to prepare them for PARCC assessments. Typically these tasks are one class period in length, and students complete them independently, without assistance. The problems should be new to the students and are not preceded by analogous problems. Teachers may use these tasks formatively or summatively.

END-OF-MODULE ASSESSMENT TASK

A summative End-of-Module Assessment Task is also provided for each module. These tasks are specifically designed based on the standards addressed in order to gauge students' full range of understanding of the module as a whole and to prepare them for PARCC assessments. Some items test understanding of specific standards, while others are synthesis items that assess either understanding of the broader concept addressed in the module or the ability to solve problems by combining knowledge, skills, and understanding. Like the mid-module tasks, these tasks are one class period in length and independently completed by the student without assistance. They also should be new to the students and not preceded by analogous problems.

Problems on these Mid-Module and End-of-Module Assessment Tasks are closely tied to the learning that takes place throughout the module. They build in complexity as the Problems Sets do in the Lessons.

RIGOR IN THE ASSESSMENTS

Each assessment encourages students to demonstrate procedural skill and conceptual understanding. Application problems, including multistep word problems, are always part of the assessments. Constructed response questions typically pose complex tasks that require students to explain their process for solving a problem. For these problems, answers alone are insufficient. Students must also be able to thoroughly explain their thought processes. Possible student work may include tape diagrams, number sentences, area models, and paragraphs. In any case, the rubrics for these items include elements on judging the thoroughness and correctness of the student's explanation.

CHAPTER 5

Approach to Differentiated Instruction

Teachers are confronted daily with meeting the needs of diverse learners in their classrooms, and differentiating instruction provides a means for meeting this challenge. This chapter explains how A *Story of Units* integrates Universal Design for Learning (UDL). Marginal notes to the teacher in lessons inform teachers about how to adapt activities to better meet the needs of various student groups.

The new standards require that "all students must have the opportunity to learn and meet the same high standards if they are to access the knowledge and skills necessary in their post-school lives." The writers of A *Story of Units* agree and feel strongly that accommodations cannot be just an extra set of resources for particular students. Instead, scaffolding must be folded into the curriculum in such a way that it is part of its very DNA. Said another way, faithful adherence to the modules is the primary scaffolding tool.

The modules that make up A *Story of Units* propose that the components of excellent math instruction do not change based on the audience. That said, specific resources within this curriculum highlight strategies that can provide critical access for all students.

Researched-based UDL has provided a structure for thinking about how to meet the needs of diverse learners. Broadly, that structure asks teachers to consider multiple means of representation, multiple means of action and expression, and multiple means of engagement. Charts at the end of this section offer suggested scaffolds, using this framework, for English language learners, students with disabilities, students performing above grade level, and students performing below grade level. UDL offers ideal settings for multiple entry points for students and minimizes instructional barriers to learning. Many of the suggestions on the chart are applicable to other students and overlapping populations.

In addition, individual lessons contain marginal notes to teachers (in text boxes) highlighting specific UDL information about scaffolds that might be employed with particular intentionality when working with students. These tips are strategically placed in the lesson where teachers might use the strategy to the best advantage.

It is important to note that the scaffolds and accommodations integrated into A *Story of Units* might change how learners access information and demonstrate learning; they do not substantially alter the instructional level, content, or performance criteria. Rather, they provide teachers with choices in how students access content and demonstrate their knowledge and ability.

We encourage teachers to pay particular attention to the manner in which knowledge is sequenced in A *Story of Units* and to capitalize on that sequence when working with special student populations. Most lessons contain a suggested teaching sequence that moves from simple to complex, starting, for example, with an introductory problem for a math topic and building up inductively to the general case encompassing multifaceted ideas. By breaking down problems from simple to complex, teachers can locate specific steps that students are struggling with or stretch out problems for students who desire a challenge.

Throughout A *Story of Units*, teachers are encouraged to give classwork using a *time* frame rather than a *task* frame. In other words, within a given time frame, all students are expected to do their personal best, working at their maximum potential: "Students, you have ten minutes to work independently." Bonus questions are always ready for accelerated students. The teacher circulates and monitors the work, error-correcting effectively and wisely. Some students complete more work in the time frame than others. Neither above- nor below-grade level students are overly praised or penalized. Personal success is what we are striving for.

Another vitally important component for meeting the needs of all students is the constant flow of data from student work. A *Story of Units* provides daily tracking through exit tickets for each lesson, as well as Mid- and End-of-Module Assessment Tasks to determine student understanding at benchmark points. These tasks should accompany teacher-made test items in a comprehensive assessment plan. Such data flow keeps teaching practice firmly grounded in student learning and makes incremental forward movement possible. A culture of precise error correction in the classroom breeds a comfort with data that is nonpunitive and honest. When feedback is provided with emotional neutrality, students understand that making mistakes is part of the learning process: "Students, for the next five minutes, I will be meeting with Brenda, Mehmet, and Jeremy. They did not remember to rename the remainder in the tens place as 10 ones in their long division on Problem 7." Conducting such sessions then provides the teacher the opportunity to quickly assess if students need to start at a simpler level or just need more monitored practice now that their eyes are open to their mistakes.

Good mathematics instruction, like any successful coaching, involves demonstration, modeling, and a lot of intelligent practice. In math, just as in sports, skill is acquired incrementally; as the student acquires greater skill, more complexity is added to the work, and the student's proficiency grows. The careful sequencing of the mathematics and the many scaffolds that have been designed into A *Story of Units* make it an excellent curriculum for meeting the needs of all students, including those with special and unique learning modes.

SCAFFOLDS FOR ENGLISH LANGUAGE LEARNERS

English language learners (ELLs) provide a variety of experiences that can add to the classroom environment. Their differences do not translate directly to shortfalls in knowledge base but rather present an opportunity to enrich the teaching and learning. The following chart provides a bank of suggestions within the UDL framework to aid ELLs. Variations on these accommodations are elaborated within lessons, demonstrating how and when they might be used.

Provide Multiple Means of Representation	• Introduce essential terms and vocabulary prior the mathematics instruction. • Clarify, compare, and make connections to math words in discussion, particularly during and after practice. • Highlight critical vocabulary in discussion. For example, show a picture of *half*. • Couple teacher-talk with math-they-can-see, such as models. • Let students use models and gestures to calculate and explain. For example, a student searching to define *multiplication* may model groups of 6 with drawings or concrete objects and write the number sentence to match. • Teach students how to ask questions (such as, "Do you agree?" and "Why do you think so?") to extend think-pair-share conversations. Model and post conversation starters, such as, "I agree because …" "Can you explain how you solved it?" "I noticed that …" "Your solution is different from [the same as] mine because …" "My mistake was to …" • Connect language (such as *tens*) with concrete and pictorial experiences (such as money and fingers).
Provide Multiple Means of Action and Expression	• Know, use, and make the most of student cultural and home experiences. Build on the student's background knowledge. • Check for understanding frequently (e.g., "Show me what you are thinking.") to benefit those who may shy away from asking questions. • Couple teacher-talk with illustrative gestures. Vary your voice to guide comprehension. Speak dynamically with expression. Make eye-to-eye contact, and speak slowly and distinctly. • Vary the grouping in the classroom, such as sometimes using small group instruction to help ELLs learn to negotiate vocabulary with classmates and other times using native language support to allow a student to find full proficiency of the mathematics first. • Provide sufficient wait time to allow the students to process the meanings in the different languages. • Listen intently in order to uncover the math content in the students' speech. • Keep teacher-talk clear and concise. • Point to visuals while speaking, using your hands to clearly indicate the image that corresponds to your words. • Get students up and moving, coupling language with motion such as, "Say *right angle*, and show me a right angle with your legs." "Make groups of 5 right now!" • Celebrate improvement. Intentionally highlight student math success frequently.
Provide Multiple Means of Engagement	• Provide a variety of ways to respond: oral, choral, student boards, concrete models (e.g., fingers), pictorial models (e.g., ten-frame), pair share, small group share. • Treat everyday and first language and experiences as resources, not as obstacles. Be aware of gerunds, such as *denominator* in English and *denominador* in Spanish. • Provide oral options for assessment rather than multiple choice. • Cultivate a math discourse of synthesis, analysis, and evaluation rather than simplified language. • Support oral or written response with sentence frames, such as, "_____ is ___ hundreds,___ tens, and ___ ones." • Ask questions to probe what students mean as they attempt expression in a second language. • Scaffold questioning to guide connections, analysis, and mastery. • Let students choose the language they prefer for arithmetic computation and discourse.

SCAFFOLDS FOR STUDENTS WITH DISABILITIES

Individualized Education Programs (IEPs) or Section 504 Accommodation Plans should be the first source of information for designing instruction for students with disabilities. The following chart provides an additional bank of suggestions within the UDL framework for strategies to use with these students in your class. Variations on these scaffolds are elaborated at particular points within lessons with text boxes at appropriate points, demonstrating how and when they might be used.

Provide Multiple Means of Representation	• Teach from simple to complex, moving from concrete to representation to abstract at the student's pace.
	• Clarify, compare, and make connections to math words in discussion, particularly during and after practice.

• Partner key words with visuals (e.g., a photo of *ticket*) and gestures (e.g., for *paid*). Connect language (such as *tens*) with concrete and pictorial experiences (such as money and fingers). Couple teacher-talk with math-they-can-see, such as models. Let students use models and gestures to calculate and explain. For example, a student searching to define *multiplication* may model groups of 6 with drawings or concrete objects and write the number sentence to match.

• Teach students how to ask questions (such as, "Do you agree?" and "Why do you think so?") to extend think-pair-share conversations. Model and post conversation starters, such as: "I agree because …" "Can you explain how you solved it?" "I noticed that …" "Your solution is different from [the same as] mine because …" "My mistake was to …"

• Couple number sentences with models. For example, for equivalent fraction sprint, present 6/8 with

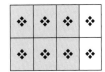

• Enlarge print for visually impaired learners.
• Use student boards to work on one calculation at a time.
• Invest in or make math picture dictionaries or word walls.

Provide Multiple Means of Action and Expression	• Provide a variety of ways to respond: oral, choral, student boards, concrete models (e.g., fingers), pictorial models (e.g., ten-frame), pair share, and small group share. For example, use student boards to adjust partner share for hearing-impaired students. Partners can jot questions and answers to one another on boards. Use vibrations or visual signs (such as a clap rather than a snap or saying, "Show") to elicit responses from hearing-impaired students.

• Vary choral response with written response (number sentences and models) on student boards to ease linguistic barriers. Support oral or written response with sentence frames, such as "_____ is ____ hundreds, _____ tens, and _____ ones."

• Adjust oral fluency games by using student and teacher boards or hand signals, such as showing the sum with fingers. Use visual signals or vibrations to elicit responses, for example, a hand pointed down means to count backward in Happy Counting (a fluency exercise).

• Adjust wait time for interpreters of hearing-impaired students.
• Select numbers and tasks that are just right for learners.
• Model each step of the algorithm before students begin.
• Give students a chance to practice the next day's sprint (fluency exercise) beforehand (e.g., at home).

• Give students a few extra minutes to process the information before giving the signal to respond.

• Assess by multiple means, including "show and tell" rather than written.

• Elaborate on the problem-solving process. Read word problems aloud. Post a visual display of the problem-solving process. Have students check off or highlight each step as they work. Talk through the problem-solving process step by step to demonstrate the thinking process. Before students solve, ask questions for comprehension, such as, "What unit are we counting? What happened to the units in the story?" Teach students to use self-questioning techniques, such as, *Does my answer make sense?*

• Concentrate on goals for accomplishment within a time frame as opposed to a task frame. Extend the time for the task. Guide students to evaluate process and practice. Have students ask themselves, *How did I improve? What did I do well?*

• Focus on students' mathematical reasoning (i.e., their ability to make comparisons, describe patterns, generalize, explain conclusions, specify claims, and use models), not their accuracy in language.

Provide Multiple Means of Engagement	• Make eye-to-eye contact, and keep teacher-talk clear and concise. Speak clearly when checking answers for sprints and problems. • Check frequently for understanding (e.g., *show*). Listen intently in order to uncover the math content in the students' speech. Use nonverbal signals, such as thumbs-up. Assign a buddy or a group to clarify directions or process. • Teach in small chunks so students get a lot of practice with one step at a time. • Know, use, and make the most of Deaf culture and sign language. • Use songs, rhymes, or rhythms to help students remember key concepts, such as, "Add your ones up first/Make a bundle if you can!" • Point to visuals and captions while speaking, using your hands to clearly indicate the image that corresponds to your words. • Incorporate activity. Get students up and moving, coupling language with motion, such as, "Say *right angle*, and show me a right angle with your legs," and "Make groups of 5 right now!" Make the most of the fun exercises for activities like sprints and fluencies. Conduct simple oral games, such as Happy Counting. Celebrate improvement. Intentionally highlight student math success frequently. • Follow predictable routines to allow students to focus on content rather than behavior. • Allow everyday and first language to express math understanding. • Reteach the same concept with a variety of fluency games. • Allow students to lead group and pair-share activities. • Provide learning aids, such as calculators and computers, to help students focus on conceptual understanding.

SCAFFOLDS FOR STUDENTS PERFORMING BELOW GRADE LEVEL

The following chart provides a bank of suggestions within the UDL framework for accommodating students who are below grade level in your class. Variations on these accommodations are elaborated within lessons, demonstrating how and when they might be used.

Provide Multiple Means of Representation	• Model problem-solving sets with drawings and graphic organizers (e.g., bar or tape diagram), giving many examples and visual displays. • Guide students as they select and practice using their own graphic organizers and models to solve. • Use direct instruction for vocabulary with visual or concrete representations. • Use explicit directions with steps and procedures enumerated. Guide students through initial practice promoting gradual independence: "I do, we do, you do." • Use alternative methods of delivery of instruction, such as recordings and videos, that can be accessed independently or repeated if necessary. • Scaffold complex concepts, and provide leveled problems for multiple entry points.
Provide Multiple Means of Action and Expression	• First use manipulatives or real objects (such as dollar bills); then make the transition from concrete to pictorial to abstract. • Have students restate their learning for the day. Ask for a different representation in the restatement: "Would you restate that answer in a different way or show me by using a diagram?" • Encourage students to explain their thinking and strategy for the solution. • Choose numbers and tasks that are just right for learners but teach the same concepts. • Adjust numbers in calculations to suit the learner's levels. For example, change 429 divided by 2 to 400 divided by 2 or 4 divided by 2.

Provide Multiple Means of Engagement	• Clearly model steps, procedures, and questions to ask when solving. • Cultivate peer-assisted learning interventions for instruction (e.g., dictation) and practice, particularly for computation work (e.g., peer modeling). Have students work together to solve and then check their solutions. • Teach students to ask themselves questions as they solve: *Do I know the meaning of all the words in this problem?; What is being asked? Do I have all of the information I need? What do I do first? What is the order to solve this problem? What calculations do I need to make?* • Practice routine to ensure smooth transitions. • Set goals with students regarding the type of math work students should complete in 60 seconds. • Set goals with the students regarding next steps and what to focus on next.

SCAFFOLDS FOR STUDENTS PERFORMING ABOVE GRADE LEVEL

The following chart provides a bank of suggestions within the UDL framework for accommodating students who are above grade level in your class. Variations on these accommodations are elaborated within lessons, demonstrating how and when they might be used.

Provide Multiple Means of Representation	• Teach students how to ask questions (such as, "Do you agree?" and "Why do you think so?") to extend think-pair-share conversations. Model and post conversation starters, such as, "I agree because …" "Can you explain how you solved it?" "I noticed that …" "Your solution is different from [the same as] mine because …" "My mistake was to …" • Incorporate written reflection, evaluation, and synthesis. • Allow creativity in expression and modeling solutions.
Provide Multiple Means of Action and Expression	• Encourage students to explain their reasoning both orally and in writing. • Extend exploration of math topics by means of challenging games, puzzles, and brain teasers. Offer choices of independent or group assignments for early finishers. • Encourage students to notice and explore patterns and to identify rules and relationships in math. Have students share their observations in discussion and writing (e.g., journaling). • Foster their curiosity about numbers and mathematical ideas. Facilitate research and exploration through discussion, experiments, Internet searches, trips, and other means. • Have students compete in a secondary simultaneous competition, such as skip counting by 75s, while peers are completing the sprint. • Let students choose their mode of response: written, oral, concrete, pictorial, or abstract. • Increase the pace. Offer two word problems to solve rather than one. Adjust the difficulty level by increasing the number of steps (e.g., change a one-step problem to a two-step problem), enhancing the operation (e.g., addition to multiplication), increasing numbers to millions, or decreasing numbers to decimals or fractions. • Let students compose their own word problems to show their mastery and extension of the content.
Provide Multiple Means of Engagement	• Push student comprehension into higher levels of Bloom's Taxonomy with questions such as, "What would happen if …?" "Can you propose an alternative?" "How would you evaluate …?" "What choice would you have made?" Ask "why?" and "what if?" questions. • Celebrate improvement in completion time (e.g., Sprint A completed in 45 seconds and Sprint B completed in 30 seconds). • Make the most of the fun exercises for practicing skip counting. • Accept and elicit student ideas and suggestions for ways to extend games. • Cultivate student persistence in problem solving, and do not overlook their need for guidance and support.

CHAPTER 6

Grade-Level Module Summary and Unpacking of Standards

Although the standards delineate what students should learn at each grade level, teachers must still fill in the blanks when it comes to translating this information for use in their daily classroom practice. Questions often remain about how concepts should be connected and where parameters should be set. The content of each grade level in *A Story of Units* is contained in five to eight modules that span an academic year.

This chapter presents key information from the modules to provide an overview of the content and explain the mathematical progression. The standards are translated for teachers and a fuller picture is drawn of the teaching and learning that should take place through the school year. Each module has these sections:

An Overview of the module

Focus Grade-Level Standards

Foundational Standards

Focus Standards for Mathematical Practice

Topic Overview narratives, coherence links, and lesson objectives

The Module Overview narrative provides a broad overview for the entire module and includes information on the sequencing of the topics. The Topic Overviews unpack the standards by providing additional details about the skills and concepts students should master at the lesson level. Further unpacking of the standards continues as the lesson objectives illuminate what students should know and be able to do to demonstrate mastery. This information, taken together for all modules, tells a story of the mathematics that students should learn for the grade level.

MODULE 1: PLACE VALUE AND DECIMAL FRACTIONS

OVERVIEW

In Module 1, a 20-day module, students' understanding of the patterns in the base-ten system is extended from their work in Grade 4 with place value of multi-digit whole numbers and decimals to the hundredths to thousandths place. In Grade 5, students deepen their knowledge through a more generalized understanding of the relationships between and among adjacent places on the place value chart—for example, 1 tenth times any digit on the place value chart moves it one place value to the right (5.NBT.1). Toward the end of the module, students apply these new understandings as they reason about and perform decimal operations through the hundredths place.

Topic A opens the module with a conceptual exploration of the multiplicative patterns of the base-ten system using place value disks and a place value chart. Students notice that multiplying by 1,000 is the same as multiplying by 10 × 10 × 10. Since each factor of 10 shifts the digits one place to the left, multiplying by 10 × 10 × 10—which can be recorded in exponential form as 10^3 (5.NBT.2)—shifts the position of the digits to the left 3 places, thus changing the digits' relationships to the decimal point (5.NBT.2). Application of these place value understandings to problem solving with metric conversions completes Topic A (5.MD.1).

Topic B moves into the naming of decimal fraction numbers in expanded, unit (e.g., 4.23 = 4 ones 2 tenths 3 hundredths), and word forms and concludes with using like units to compare decimal fractions. Now in Grade 5, students use exponents and the unit fraction to represent expanded form, for example, $2 \times 10^2 + 3 \times (1/10) + 4 \times (1/100) = 200.34$ (5.NBT.3). Furthermore, students reason about differences in the values of like place value units and expressing those comparisons with symbols (>, <, and =). Students generalize their knowledge of rounding whole numbers to round decimal numbers in Topic C, initially using a vertical number line to interpret the result as an approximation and eventually moving away from the visual model (5.NBT.4).

In the remaining topics of Module 1, students use the relationships of adjacent units and generalize whole number algorithms to decimal fraction operations (5.NBT.7). Topic D uses unit form to connect general methods for addition and subtraction with whole numbers to decimal addition and subtraction; for example, 7 tens + 8 tens = 15 tens = 150 is analogous to 7 tenths + 8 tenths = 15 tenths = 1.5.

Topic E bridges the gap between Grade 4 work with multiplication and the standard algorithm by focusing on an intermediate step—reasoning about multiplying a decimal by a one-digit whole number. The area model, with which students have had extensive experience since Grade 3, is used as a scaffold for this work.

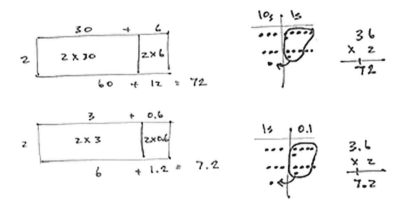

Topic F concludes Module 1 with a similar exploration of division of decimal numbers by one-digit whole number divisors. Students solidify their skills with an understanding of the algorithm before moving on to long division involving two-digit divisors in Module 2.

The Mid-Module Assessment follows Topic C. The End-of-Module Assessment follows Topic F.

FOCUS GRADE-LEVEL STANDARDS

Understand the place value system.

5.NBT.1 Recognize that in a multi-digit number, a digit in one place represents 10 times as much as it represents in the place to its right and 1/10 of what it represents in the place to its left.

5.NBT.2 Explain patterns in the number of zeros of the product when multiplying a number by powers of 10, and explain patterns in the placement of the decimal point when a decimal is multiplied or divided by a power of 10. Use whole-number exponents to denote powers of 10.

5.NBT.3 Read, write, and compare decimals to thousandths.

   a. Read and write decimals to thousandths using base-ten numerals, number names, and expanded form, e.g., $347.392 = 3 \times 100 + 4 \times 10 + 7 \times 1 + 3 \times (1/10) + 9 \times (1/100) + 2 \times (1/1000)$.

   b. Compare two decimals to thousandths based on meanings of the digits in each place, using >, =, and < symbols to record the results of comparisons.

5.NBT.4 Use place value understanding to round decimals to any place.

Perform operations with multi-digit whole numbers and with decimals to hundredths.[1]

5.NBT.7 Add, subtract, multiply, and divide decimals to hundredths, using concrete models or drawings and strategies based on place value, properties of operations, and/or the relationship between addition and subtraction; relate the strategy to a written method and explain the reasoning used.

Convert like measurement units within a given measurement system.

5.MD.1 Convert among different-sized standard measurement units within a given measurement system (e.g., convert 5 cm to 0.05 m), and use these conversions in solving multistep, real world problems.[2]

FOUNDATIONAL STANDARDS

4.NBT.1 Recognize that in a multi-digit whole number, a digit in one place represents 10 times what it represents in the place to its right. *For example, recognize that 700 ÷ 70 = 10 by applying concepts of place value and division.*

4.NBT.3 Use place value understanding to round multi-digit whole numbers to any place.

4.NF.5 Express a fraction with denominator 10 as an equivalent fraction with denominator 100, and use this technique to add two fractions with respective denominators 10 and 100. (Students who can generate equivalent fractions can develop strategies for adding fractions with unlike denominators in general. But addition and subtraction with unlike denominators in general is not a requirement at this grade.) For example, express 3/10 as 30/100, and add 3/10 + 4/100 = 34/100.

4.NF.6 Use decimal notation for fractions with denominators 10 or 100. *For example, rewrite 0.62 as 62/100; describe a length as 0.62 meters; locate 0.62 on a number line diagram.*

4.NF.7 Compare two decimals to hundredths by reasoning about their size. Recognize that comparisons are valid only when the two decimals refer to the same whole. Record the results of comparisons with the symbols >, =, or <, and justify the conclusions, e.g., by using a visual model.

4.MD.1 Know relative sizes of measurement units within one system of units including km, m, cm; kg, g; lb, oz.; l, ml; hr, min, sec. Within a single system of measurement, express measurements in a larger unit in terms of a smaller unit. Record measurement equivalents in a two-column table. For example, know that 1 ft is 12 times as long as 1 in. Express the length of a 4 ft snake as 48 in. Generate a conversion table for feet and inches listing the number pairs (1, 12), (2, 24), (3, 36), . . .

4.MD.2 Use the four operations to solve word problems involving distances, intervals of time, liquid volumes, masses of objects, and money, including problems involving simple fractions or decimals, and problems that require expressing measurements given in a larger unit in terms of a smaller unit. Represent measurement quantities using diagrams such as number line diagrams that feature a measurement scale.

FOCUS STANDARDS FOR MATHEMATICAL PRACTICE

MP.6 *Attend to precision.* Students express the units of the base-ten system as they work with decimal operations, expressing decompositions and compositions with understanding, for example, "9 hundredths + 4 hundredths = 13 hundredths. I can change 10 hundredths to make 1 tenth."

MP.7 *Look for and make use of structure.* Students explore the multiplicative patterns of the base-ten system when they use place value charts and disks to highlight the relationships between adjacent places. Students also use patterns to name decimal fraction numbers in expanded, unit, and word forms.

MP.8 *Look for and express regularity in repeated reasoning.* Students express regularity in repeated reasoning when they look for and use whole number general methods to add and subtract decimals and when they multiply and divide decimals by whole numbers. Students also use powers of 10 to explain patterns in the placement of the decimal point and generalize their knowledge of rounding whole numbers to round decimal numbers.

MODULE TOPIC SUMMARIES

Topic A: Multiplicative Patterns on the Place Value Chart

Topic A begins with a conceptual exploration of the multiplicative patterns of the base-ten system. This exploration extends the place value work done with multi-digit whole numbers in Grade 4 to larger multi-digit whole numbers and decimals. Students use place value disks and a place value chart to build the place value chart from millions to thousandths. They compose and decompose units crossing the decimal with a view toward extending students' knowledge of the 10 *times as large* and $\frac{1}{10}$ *as large* relationships among whole number places to that of adjacent decimal places. This concrete experience is linked to the effects on the product when multiplying any number by a power of 10. For example, students notice that multiplying 0.4 by 1,000 shifts the position of the digits to the left 3 places, changing the digits' relationships to the decimal point and producing a product with a value that is $10 \times 10 \times 10$ as large (400.0) (5.NBT.2). Students explain these changes in value and shifts in position in terms of place value. In addition, they learn a new and more efficient way to represent place value units using exponents—for example, 1 thousand = 1,000 = 10^3 (5.NBT.2). Conversions among metric units such as kilometers, meters, and centimeters give an opportunity to apply these extended place value relationships and exponents in a meaningful context by exploring word problems in the last lesson of Topic A (5.MD.1).

Focus Standard:	5.NBT.1	Recognize that in a multi-digit number, a digit in one place represents 10 times as much as it represents in the place to its right and 1/10 of what it represents in the place to its left.
	5.NBT.2	Explain patterns in the number of zeros of the product when multiplying a number by powers of 10, and explain patterns in the placement of the decimal point when a decimal is multiplied or divided by a power of 10. Use whole-number exponents to denote powers of 10.
	5.MD.1	Convert among different-sized standard measurement units within a given measurement system (e.g., convert 5 cm to 0.05 m), and use these conversions in solving multistep, real world problems.
Instructional Days:	4	
Coherence		
Links from:	G4–M1	Place Value, Rounding, and Algorithms for Addition and Subtraction
Links to:	G6–M2	Arithmetic Operations Including Dividing by a Fraction

Objective 1: Reason concretely and pictorially using place value understanding to relate adjacent base-ten units from millions to thousandths.
(Lesson 1)

Objective 2: Reason abstractly using place value understanding to relate adjacent base-ten units from millions to thousandths.
(Lesson 2)

Objective 3: Use exponents to name place value units and explain patterns in the placement of the decimal point.
(Lesson 3)

Objective 4: Use exponents to denote powers of 10 with application to metric conversions.
(Lesson 4)

Topic B: Decimal Fractions and Place Value Patterns

Naming decimal fractions in expanded, unit, and word forms in order to compare decimal fractions is the focus of Topic B (5.NBT.3). Familiar methods of expressing expanded form are used, but students are also encouraged to apply their knowledge of exponents to expanded forms (e.g., $4{,}300.01 = 4 \times 10^3 + 3 \times 10^2 + 1 \times \frac{1}{100}$). Place value charts and disks offer a beginning for comparing decimal fractions to the thousandths, but they are quickly supplanted by reasoning about the meaning of the digits in each place and noticing differences in the values of like units and expressing those comparisons with symbols (>, <, and =).

Focus Standard:	5.NBT.3	Read, write, and compare decimals to thousandths.
		a. Read and write decimals to thousandths using base-ten numerals, number names, and expanded form, e.g., 347.392 = 3 × 100 + 4 × 10 + 7 × 1 + 3 × (1/10) + 9 × (1/100) + 2 × (1/1000).
		b. Compare two decimals to thousandths based on meanings of the digits in each place, using >, =, and < symbols to record the results of comparisons.
Instructional Days:	2	
Coherence		
Links from:	G4–M1	Place Value, Rounding, and Algorithms for Addition and Subtraction
Links to:	G6–M2	Arithmetic Operations Including Dividing by a Fraction

Objective 1: Name decimal fractions in expanded, unit, and word forms by applying place value reasoning.
(Lesson 5)

Objective 2: Compare decimal fractions to the thousandths using like units and express comparisons with >, <, =.
(Lesson 6)

Topic C: Place Value and Rounding Decimal Fractions

Students generalize their knowledge of rounding whole numbers to round decimal numbers to any place in Topic C. In Grades 2 and 4, vertical number lines provided a platform for students to round whole numbers to any place. In Grade 5, vertical number lines again provide support for students to make use of patterns in the base-ten system, allowing knowledge of whole number rounding (4.NBT.3) to be easily applied to rounding decimal values (5.NBT.4). The vertical number line is used initially to find more than or less than halfway between multiples of decimal units. In Lesson 8, students are encouraged to reason more abstractly as they use place value understanding to approximate by using nearest multiples. Naming those nearest multiples is an application of flexibly naming decimals using like place value units. To round 53.805 (53 ones 805 thousandths) to the nearest hundredth, students find the nearest multiples, 53.800 (53 ones 800 thousandths) and 53.810 (53 ones 810 thousandths), and then decide that 53.805 is exactly halfway between and therefore must be rounded up to 53.810.

Focus Standard:	5.NBT.4	Use place value understanding to round decimals to any place.
Instructional Days:	2	
Coherence		
Links from:	G4–M1	Place Value, Rounding, and Algorithms for Addition and Subtraction
Links to:	G6–M2	Arithmetic Operations Including Dividing by a Fraction

Objective 1: Round a given decimal to any place using place value understanding and the vertical number line.
(Lessons 7 and 8)

Topic D: Adding and Subtracting Decimals

Topics D through F mark a shift from the opening topics of Module 1. From this point to the conclusion of the module, students begin to use base-ten understanding of adjacent units and whole number algorithms to reason about and perform decimal fraction operations:

addition and subtraction in Topic D, multiplication in Topic E, and division in Topic F (5. NBT.7). In Topic D, unit form provides the connection that allows students to use what they know about general methods for addition and subtraction with whole numbers to reason about decimal addition and subtraction, for example, 7 tens + 8 tens = 15 tens = 150 is analogous to 7 tenths + 8 tenths = 15 tenths = 1.5. Place value charts and disks (both concrete and pictorial representations) and the relationship between addition and subtraction are used to provide a bridge for relating such understandings to a written method. Real-world contexts provide opportunity for students to apply their knowledge of decimal addition and subtraction as well in Topic D.

Focus Standard:	5.NBT.2	Explain patterns in the number of zeros of the product when multiplying a number by powers of 10, and explain patterns in the placement of the decimal point when a decimal is multiplied or divided by a power of 10. Use whole-number exponents to denote powers of 10.
	5.NBT.3	Read, write, and compare decimals to thousandths.
		a. Read and write decimals to thousandths using base-ten numerals, number names, and expanded form, e.g., $347.392 = 3 \times 100 + 4 \times 10 + 7 \times 1 + 3 \times (1/10) + 9 \times (1/100) + 2 \times (1/1000)$.
		b. Compare two decimals to thousandths based on meanings of the digits in each place, using >, =, and < symbols to record the results of comparisons.
	5.NBT.7	Add, subtract, multiply and divide decimals to hundredths, using concrete models or drawings and strategies based on place value, properties of operations, and/or the relationship between addition and subtraction; relate the strategy to a written method and explain the reasoning used.
Instructional Days:	2	
Coherence		
Links from:	G4–M1	Place Value, Rounding, and Algorithms for Addition and Subtraction
Links to:	G6–M2	Arithmetic Operations Including Dividing by a Fraction

Objective 1: Add decimals using place value strategies and relate those strategies to a written method.
(Lesson 9)

Objective 2: Subtract decimals using place value strategies and relate those strategies to a written method.
(Lesson 10)

Topic E: Multiplying Decimals

A focus on reasoning about the multiplication of a decimal fraction by a one-digit whole number in Topic E provides the link that connects Grade 4 multiplication work and Grade 5 fluency with multi-digit multiplication. Place value understanding of whole number multiplication coupled with an area model of the distributive property is used to help students build direct parallels between whole number products and the products of one-digit multipliers and decimals (5.NBT.7). Students use an estimation-based strategy to confirm the reasonableness of the product once the decimal has been placed through place value reasoning. Word problems provide a context within which students can reason about products.

Focus Standard:	5.NBT.2	Explain patterns in the number of zeros of the product when multiplying a number by powers of 10, and explain patterns in the placement of the decimal point when a decimal is multiplied or divided by a power of 10. Use whole-number exponents to denote powers of 10.
	5.NBT.3	Read, write, and compare decimals to thousandths.
		a. Read and write decimals to thousandths using base-ten numerals, number names, and expanded form, e.g., $347.392 = 3 \times 100 + 4 \times 10 + 7 \times 1 + 3 \times (1/10) + 9 \times (1/100) + 2 \times (1/1000)$.
		b. Compare two decimals to thousandths based on meanings of the digits in each place, using >, =, and < symbols to record the results of comparisons.
	5.NBT.7	Add, subtract, multiply, and divide decimals to hundredths, using concrete models or drawings and strategies based on place value, properties of operations, and/or the relationship between addition and subtraction; relate the strategy to a written method and explain the reasoning used.
Instructional Days:	2	
Coherence		
Links from:	G4–M3	Multi-Digit Multiplication and Division
Links to:	G5–M2	Multi-Digit Whole Number and Decimal Fraction Operations
	G6–M2	Arithmetic Operations Including Dividing by a Fraction

Objective 1: Multiply a decimal fraction by single-digit whole numbers, relate to a written method through application of the area model and place value understanding, and explain the reasoning used.
(Lesson 11)

Objective 2: Multiply a decimal fraction by single-digit whole numbers, including using estimation to confirm the placement of the decimal point.
(Lesson 12)

Topic F: Dividing Decimals

Topic F concludes Module 1 with an exploration of division of decimal numbers by one-digit whole number divisors using place value charts and disks. Lessons begin with easily identifiable multiples such as $4.2 \div 6$ and move to quotients that have a remainder in the smallest unit (through the thousandths). Written methods for decimal cases are related to place value strategies, properties of operations, and familiar written methods for whole numbers (5.NBT.7). Students solidify their skills with an understanding of the algorithm before moving on to division involving two-digit divisors in Module 2. Students apply their accumulated knowledge of decimal operations to solve word problems at the close of the module.

Focus Standard:	5.NBT.3	Read, write, and compare decimals to thousandths.
		a. Read and write decimals to thousandths using base-ten numerals, number names, and expanded form, e.g., $347.392 = 3 \times 100 + 4 \times 10 + 7 \times 1 + 3 \times (1/10) + 9 \times (1/100) + 2 \times (1/1000)$.
		b. Compare two decimals to thousandths based on meanings of the digits in each place, using >, =, and < symbols to record the results of comparisons.
	5.NBT.7	Add, subtract, multiply, and divide decimals to hundredths, using concrete models or drawings and strategies based on place value, properties of operations, and/or the relationship between addition and subtraction; relate the strategy to a written method and explain the reasoning used.
Instructional Days:	4	

Coherence		
Links from:	G4–M3	Multi-Digit Multiplication and Division
Links to:	G5–M2	Multi-Digit Whole Number and Decimal Fraction Operations
	G6–M2	Arithmetic Operations Including Dividing by a Fraction

Objective 1: Divide decimals by single-digit whole numbers involving easily identifiable multiples using place value understanding and relate to a written method.
(Lesson 13)

Objective 2: Divide decimals with a remainder using place value understanding and relate to a written method.
(Lesson 14)

Objective 3: Divide decimals using place value understanding including remainders in the smallest unit.
(Lesson 15)

Objective 4: Solve word problems using decimal operations.
(Lesson 16)

MODULE 2: MULTI-DIGIT WHOLE NUMBER AND DECIMAL FRACTION OPERATIONS

OVERVIEW

In Module 1, students explored the relationships of adjacent units on the place value chart to generalize whole number algorithms to decimal fraction operations. In Module 2, a 35-day module, students apply the patterns of the base-ten system to mental strategies and the multiplication and division algorithms.

Topics A through D provide a sequential study of multiplication. To link to prior learning and set the foundation for understanding the standard multiplication algorithm, students begin at the concrete–pictorial level in Topic A. They use number disks to model multi-digit multiplication of place value units, for example, 42 × 10, 42 × 100, 42 × 1,000, leading to problems such as 42 × 30, 42 × 300 and 42 × 3,000 (5.NBT.1, 5.NBT.2). They then round factors in Lesson 2 and discuss the reasonableness of their products. Throughout Topic A, students evaluate and write simple expressions to record their calculations using the associative property and parentheses to record the relevant order of calculations (5.OA.1).

In Topic B, place value understanding moves toward understanding the distributive property via area diagrams, which are used to generate and record the partial products (5.OA.1, 5.OA.2) of the standard algorithm (5.NBT.5). Topic C moves students from whole numbers to multiplication with decimals, again using place value as a guide to reason and make estimations about products (5.NBT.7). In Topic D, students explore multiplication as a method for expressing equivalent measures. For example, they multiply to convert between meters and centimeters or ounces and cups with measurements in both whole number and decimal form (5.MD.1).

Topics E through H provide a similar sequence for division. Topic E begins concretely with number disks as an introduction to division with multi-digit whole numbers (5.NBT.6).

In the same lesson, 420 ÷ 60 is interpreted as 420 ÷ 10 ÷ 6. Next, students round dividends and two-digit divisors to nearby multiples of 10 in order to estimate single-digit quotients (e.g., 431 ÷ 58 ≈ 420 ÷ 60 = 7) and then multi-digit quotients. This work is done horizontally, outside the context of the written vertical method. The series of lessons in Topic F leads students to divide multi-digit dividends by two-digit divisors using the written vertical method. Each lesson moves to a new level of difficulty with a sequence beginning with divisors that are multiples of 10 to nonmultiples of 10. Two instructional days are devoted to single-digit quotients with and without remainders before progressing to two- and three-digit quotients (5.NBT.6).

In Topic G, students use their understanding to divide decimals by two-digit divisors in a sequence similar to that of Topic F with whole numbers (5.NBT.7). In Topic H, students apply the work of the module to solve multistep word problems using multi-digit division with unknowns representing either the group size or number of groups. In this topic, an emphasis on checking the reasonableness of their answers draws on skills learned throughout the module, including refining their knowledge of place value, rounding, and estimation.

FOCUS GRADE-LEVEL STANDARDS

Write and interpret numerical expressions.

5.OA.1 Use parentheses, brackets, or braces in numerical expressions, and evaluate expressions with these symbols.

5.OA.2 Write simple expressions that record calculations with numbers, and interpret numerical expressions without evaluating them. *For example, express the calculation "add 8 and 7, then multiply by 2" as 2 × (8 + 7). Recognize that 3 × (18,932 + 921) is three times as large as 18,932 + 921, without having to calculate the indicated sum or product.*

Understand the place value system.[3]

5.NBT.1 Recognize that in a multi-digit number, a digit in one place represents 10 times as much as it represents in the place to its right and 1/10 of what it represents in the place to its left.

5.NBT.2 Explain patterns in the number of zeros of the product when multiplying a number by powers of 10, and explain patterns in the placement of the decimal point when a decimal is multiplied or divided by a power of 10. Use whole-number exponents to denote power of 10.

Perform operations with multi-digit whole numbers and with decimals to hundredths.

5.NBT.5 Fluently multiply multi-digit whole numbers using the standard algorithm.

5.NBT.6 Find whole-number quotients of whole numbers with up to four-digit dividends and two-digit divisors, using strategies based on place value, the properties of operations, and/or the relationship between multiplication and division. Illustrate and explain the calculation by using equations, rectangular arrays, and/or area models.

5.NBT.7 Add, subtract, multiply, and divide decimals to hundredths, using concrete models or drawings and strategies based on place value, properties of operations, and/or the relationship between addition and subtraction; relate the strategy to a written method and explain the reasoning used.[4]

Convert like measurement units within a given measurement system.

5.MD.1 Convert among different-sized standard measurement units within a given measurement system (e.g., convert 5 cm to 0.05 m), and use these conversions in solving multistep, real world problems.

FOUNDATIONAL STANDARDS

4.OA.1 Interpret a multiplication equation as a comparison, e.g., interpret $35 = 5 \times 7$ as a statement that 35 is 5 times as many as 7 and 7 times as many as 5. Represent verbal statements of multiplicative comparisons as multiplication equations.

4.OA.3 Solve multistep word problems posed with whole numbers and having whole-number answers using the four operations, including problems in which remainders must be interpreted. Represent these problems using equations with a letter standing for the unknown quantity. Assess the reasonableness of answers using mental computation and estimation strategies including rounding.

4.NBT.4 Fluently add and subtract multi-digit whole numbers using the standard algorithm.

4.NBT.5 Multiply a whole number of up to four digits by a one-digit whole number, and multiply two two-digit numbers, using strategies based on place value and the properties of operations. Illustrate and explain the calculation by using equations, rectangular arrays, and/or area models.

4.NBT.6 Find whole-number quotients and remainders with up to four-digit dividends and one-digit divisors, using strategies based on place value, the properties of operations, and/or the relationship between multiplication and division. Illustrate and explain the calculation by using equations, rectangular arrays, and/or area models.

FOCUS STANDARDS FOR MATHEMATICAL PRACTICE

MP.1 _Make sense of problems and persevere in solving them._ Students make sense of problems when they use number disks and area models to conceptualize and solve multiplication and division problems.

MP.2 _Reason abstractly and quantitatively._ Students make sense of quantities and their relationships when they use both mental strategies and the standard algorithms to multiply and divide multi-digit whole numbers. Student also decontextualize when they represent problems symbolically and contextualize when they consider the value of the units used and understand the meaning of the quantities as they compute.

MP.7 *Look for and make use of structure.* Students apply the *times 10, 100, 1,000* and the *divide by 10* patterns of the base-ten system to mental strategies and the multiplication and division algorithms as they multiply and divide whole numbers and decimals.

MP.8 *Look for and express regularity in repeated reasoning.* Students express the regularity they notice in repeated reasoning when they apply the partial quotients algorithm to divide two-, three-, and four-digit dividends by two-digit divisors. Students also check the reasonableness of the intermediate results of their division algorithms as they solve multi-digit division word problems.

MODULE TOPIC SUMMARIES

Topic A: *Mental Strategies for Multi-Digit Whole Number Multiplication*

Topic A begins a sequential study of multiplication that culminates in Topic D. In order to link prior learning from Module 1 in both Grades 4 and 5 and set the stage for solidifying the standard multiplication algorithm, students begin at the concrete-pictorial level. They use number disks to model multi-digit multiplication of place value units, for example, 42 × 10, 42 × 100, 42 × 1,000, leading quickly to problems such as 42 × 30, 42 × 300, and 42 × 3,000 (5.NBT.1, 5.NBT.2). Students then round factors in Lesson 2 and discuss the reasonableness of their products. Throughout Topic A, students evaluate and write simple expressions to record their calculations using the associative property and parentheses to record the relevant order of calculations (5.OA.1).

Focus Standard:	5.NBT.1	Recognize that in a multi-digit number, a digit in one place represents 10 times as much as it represents in the place to its right and 1/10 of what it represents in the place to its left.
	5.NBT.2	Explain patterns in the number of zeros of the product when multiplying a number by powers of 10, and explain patterns in the placement of the decimal point when a decimal is multiplied or divided by a power of 10. Use whole-number exponents to denote power of 10.
Instructional Days:	2	
Coherence		
Links from:	G4–M3	Multi-Digit Multiplication and Division
Links to:	G5–M5	Addition and Multiplication with Volume and Area
	G6–M5	Area, Surface Area, and Volume Problems

Objective 1: Multiply multi-digit whole numbers and multiples of 10 using place value patterns and the distributive and associative properties.
(Lesson 1)

Objective 2: Estimate multi-digit products by rounding factors to a basic fact and using place value patterns.
(Lesson 2)

Topic B: *The Standard Algorithm for Multi-Digit Whole Number Multiplication*

In Topic B, place value understanding moves toward understanding the distributive property by using area diagrams to generate and record partial products (5.OA.1, 5.OA.2), which are combined within the standard algorithm (5.NBT.5). Writing and interpreting numerical expressions in Lesson 3, and comparing those expressions using visual models lay the necessary foundation for students to make connections between the distributive property as depicted in area models and the partial products within the standard multiplication algorithm. The algorithm is built over a period of days, increasing in complexity as the number of digits in both factors increases. Reasoning about zeros in the multiplier along with considerations about the reasonableness of products also provides opportunities to deepen understanding of the standard algorithm. Although word problems provide context throughout Topic B, Lesson 9's concentration of multistep problems allows students to apply this new knowledge.

Focus Standard:	5.OA.2	Write simple expressions that record calculations with numbers, and interpret numerical expressions without evaluating them. *For example, express the calculation "add 8 and 7, then multiply by 2" as 2 × (8 + 7). Recognize that 3 × (18,932 + 921) is three times as large as 18,932 + 921, without having to calculate the indicated sum or product.*
	5.NBT.5	Fluently multiply multi-digit whole numbers using the standard algorithm.
Instructional Days:	7	
Coherence		
Links from:	G4–M3	Multi-Digit Multiplication and Division
Links to:	G6–M2	Arithmetic Operations Including Dividing by a Fraction
	G6–M4	Expressions and Equations

Objective 1: Write and interpret numerical expressions, and compare expressions using a visual model.
(Lesson 3)

Objective 2: Convert numerical expressions into unit form as a mental strategy for multi-digit multiplication.
(Lesson 4)

Objective 3: Connect visual models and the distributive property to partial products of the standard algorithm without renaming.
(Lesson 5)

Objective 4: Connect area diagrams and the distributive property to partial products of the standard algorithm without renaming.
(Lesson 6)

Objective 5: Connect area diagrams and the distributive property to partial products of the standard algorithm with renaming.
(Lesson 7)

Objective 6: Fluently multiply multi-digit whole numbers using the standard algorithm and using estimation to check for reasonableness of the product.
(Lesson 8)

Objective 7: Fluently multiply multi-digit whole numbers using the standard algorithm to solve multistep word problems.
(Lesson 9)

Topic C: Decimal Multi-Digit Multiplication

Throughout Topic C, students make connections between what they know of whole number multiplication to its parallel role in multiplication with decimals by using place value to reason and make estimations about products (5.NBT.7). Knowledge of multiplicative patterns from Grade 4 experiences, as well as those in Module 1, provide support for converting decimal multiplication to whole number multiplication. Students reason about how products of such converted cases must be adjusted through division, giving rise to explanations about how the decimal must be placed.

Focus Standard:	5.NBT.7	Add, subtract, multiply, and divide decimals to hundredths, using concrete models or drawings and strategies based on place value, properties of operations, and/or the relationship between addition and subtraction; relate the strategy to a written method and explain the reasoning used.
Instructional Days:	3	
Coherence		
Links from:	G5–M1	Place Value and Decimal Fractions
Links to:	G5–M4	Multiplication and Division of Fractions and Decimal Fractions
	G6–M2	Arithmetic Operations Including Dividing by a Fraction

Objective 1: Multiply decimal fractions with tenths by multi-digit whole numbers using place value understanding to record partial products.
(Lesson 10)

Objective 2: Multiply decimal fractions by multi-digit whole numbers through conversion to a whole number problem and reasoning about the placement of the decimal.
(Lesson 11)

Objective 3: Reason about the product of a whole number and a decimal with hundredths using place value understanding and estimation.
(Lesson 12)

Topic D: Measurement Word Problems with Whole Number and Decimal Multiplication

In Topic D, students explore multiplication as a method for expressing equivalent measures. For example, they multiply to convert between meters and centimeters or ounces and cups with measurements in both whole number and decimal form (5.MD.1). These conversions offer opportunity for students to not only apply their newly found knowledge of multi-digit multiplication of both whole and decimal numbers, but also to reason deeply about the relationships between unit size and quantity—how the choice of one affects the other.

Focus Standard:	5.NBT.5	Fluently multiply multi-digit whole numbers using the standard algorithm.
	5.NBT.7	Add, subtract, multiply, and divide decimals to hundredths, using concrete models or drawings and strategies based on place value, properties of operations, and/or the relationship between addition and subtraction; relate the strategy to a written method and explain the reasoning used.
	5.MD.1	Convert among different-sized standard measurement units within a given measurement system (e.g., convert 5 cm to 0.05 m), and use these conversions in solving multistep, real world problems.
Instructional Days:	3	
Coherence		
Links from:	G4–M2	Unit Conversions and Problem Solving with Metric Measurement
Links to:	G5–M4	Multiplication and Division of Fractions and Decimal Fractions
	G6–M1	Ratios and Unit Rates

Objective 1: Use whole number multiplication to express equivalent measurements.
(Lesson 13)

Objective 2: Use decimal multiplication to express equivalent measurements.
(Lesson 14)

Objective 3: Solve two-step word problems involving measurement and multi-digit multiplication.
(Lesson 15)

Topic E: Mental Strategies for Multi-Digit Whole Number Division

Topics E through H provide a parallel sequence for division to that offered in Topics A to D for multiplication. Topic E begins concretely with number disks as an introduction to division with multi-digit whole numbers (5.NBT.6). In the same lesson, 420 ÷ 60 is interpreted as 420 ÷ 10 ÷ 6. Next, students round dividends and two-digit divisors to nearby multiples of ten in order to estimate single-digit quotients (e.g., 431 ÷ 58 ≈ 420 ÷ 60 = 7) and then multi-digit quotients. This work is done horizontally, outside the context of the written vertical method.

Focus Standard:	5.NBT.1	Recognize that in a multi-digit number, a digit in one place represents 10 times as much as it represents in the place to its right and 1/10 of what it represents in the place to its left.
	5.NBT.6	Find whole-number quotients of whole numbers with up to four-digit dividends and two-digit divisors, using strategies based on place value, the properties of operations, and/or the relationship between multiplication and division. Illustrate and explain the calculation by using equations, rectangular arrays, and/or area models.
Instructional Days:	3	
Coherence		
Links from:	G4–M3	Multi-Digit Multiplication and Division
	G5–M1	Place Value and Decimal Fractions
Links to:	G5–M4	Multiplication and Division of Fractions and Decimal Fractions
	G6–M2	Arithmetic Operations Including Dividing by a Fraction

Objective 1: Use divide by 10 patterns for multi-digit whole number division.
(Lesson 16)

Objective 2: Use basic facts to approximate quotients with two-digit divisors.
(Lessons 17 and 18)

Topic F: Partial Quotients and Multi-Digit Whole Number Division

The series of lessons in Topic F leads students to divide multi-digit dividends by two-digit divisors using the written vertical method. Each lesson moves to a new level of difficulty with a sequence beginning with divisors that are multiples of 10 to nonmultiples of 10. Two instructional days are devoted to single-digit quotients with and without remainders before progressing into two- and three-digit quotients (5.NBT.6).

Focus Standard:	5.NBT.6	Find whole-number quotients of whole numbers with up to four-digit dividends and two-digit divisors, using strategies based on place value, the properties of operations, and/or the relationship between multiplication and division. Illustrate and explain the calculation by using equations, rectangular arrays, and/or area models.
Instructional Days:	5	
Coherence		
Links from:	G4–M3	Multi-Digit Multiplication and Division
Links to:	G6–M2	Arithmetic Operations Including Dividing by a Fraction

Objective 1: Divide two- and three-digit dividends by multiples of 10 with single-digit quotients, and make connections to a written method.
(Lesson 19)

Objective 2: Divide two- and three-digit dividends by two-digit divisors with single-digit quotients, and make connections to a written method.
(Lessons 20 and 21)

Objective 3: Divide three- and four-digit dividends by two-digit divisors resulting in two- and three-digit quotients, reasoning about the decomposition of successive remainders in each place value.
(Lessons 22 and 23)

Topic G: Partial Quotients and Multi-Digit Decimal Division

Topic G uses the knowledge students have accumulated about whole number division with double-digit divisors and extends it to division of decimals by double-digit divisors (5.NBT.7). Parallels between sharing or grouping whole number units, and sharing or grouping decimal units are the emphasis of Topic G. Students quickly surmise that the concepts of division remain the same regardless of the size of the units being shared or grouped. Placement of the decimal point in quotients is based on students' reasoning about when wholes are being shared or grouped and when the part being shared or grouped transitions into fractional parts. Students reason about remainders in a deeper way than in previous grades. They also consider cases in which remainders expressed as whole numbers appear to be equivalent; however, equivalence is disproven when such remainders are decomposed as decimal units and shared or grouped.

Focus Standard:	5.NBT.7	Add, subtract, multiply, and divide decimals to hundredths, using concrete models or drawings and strategies based on place value, properties of operations, and/or the relationship between addition and subtraction; relate the strategy to a written method and explain the reasoning used.
Instructional Days:	4	
Coherence		
Links from:	G5–M1	Place Value and Decimal Fractions
Links to:	G6–M2	Arithmetic Operations Including Dividing by a Fraction

Objective 1: Divide decimal dividends by multiples of 10, reasoning about the placement of the decimal point and making connections to a written method.
(Lesson 24)

Objective 2: Use basic facts to approximate decimal quotients with two-digit divisors, reasoning about the placement of the decimal point.
(Lesson 25)

Objective 3: Divide decimal dividends by two-digit divisors, estimating quotients, reasoning about the placement of the decimal point, and making connections to a written method.
(Lessons 26 and 27)

Topic H: Measurement Word Problems with Multi-Digit Division

In Topic H, students apply the work of the module to solve multistep word problems using multi-digit division (5.NBT.6). Cases include unknowns representing either the group size or number of groups. In this topic, an emphasis on checking the reasonableness of their solutions draws on skills learned throughout the module, which includes using knowledge of place value, rounding, and estimation. Students relate calculations to reasoning about division through a variety of strategies, including place value, properties of operations, equations, and area models.

Focus Standard:	5.NBT.6	Find whole-number quotients of whole numbers with up to four-digit dividends and two-digit divisors, using strategies based on place value, the properties of operations, and/or the relationship between multiplication and division. Illustrate and explain the calculation by using equations, rectangular arrays, and/or area models.
Instructional Days:	2	
Coherence		
Links from:	G4–M3	Multi-Digit Multiplication and Division
Links to:	G6–M2	Arithmetic Operations Including Dividing by a Fraction

Objective 1: Solve division word problems involving multi-digit division with group size unknown and the number of groups unknown.
(Lessons 28 and 29)

MODULE 3: ADDITION AND SUBTRACTION OF FRACTIONS

OVERVIEW

In Module 3, which extends 22 days, students' understanding of addition and subtraction of fractions extends from earlier work with fraction equivalence and decimals. This module marks a significant shift away from the elementary grades' centrality of base-ten units to the study and use of the full set of fractional units from Grade 5 forward, especially as applied to algebra.

In Topic A, students revisit the foundational Grade 4 standards addressing equivalence. When equivalent, fractions represent the same amount of area of a rectangle, the same point on the number line. These equivalencies can also be represented symbolically.

$$\frac{2}{3} = \frac{2 \times 4}{3 \times 4} = \frac{8}{12}$$

Furthermore, equivalence is evidenced when adding fractions with the same denominator. The sum may be decomposed into parts (or recomposed into an equal sum)—for example:

$$\frac{2}{3} = \frac{1}{3} + \frac{1}{3}$$

$$\frac{7}{8} = \frac{3}{8} + \frac{3}{8} + \frac{1}{8}$$

$$\frac{6}{2} = \frac{2}{2} + \frac{2}{2} + \frac{2}{2} = 1 + 1 + 1 = 3$$

$$\frac{8}{5} = \frac{5}{5} + \frac{3}{5} = 1\frac{3}{5}$$

$$\frac{7}{3} = \frac{6}{3} + \frac{1}{3} = 2 \times \frac{3}{3} + \frac{1}{3} = 2 + \frac{1}{3} = 2\frac{1}{3}$$

This is also carrying forward work with decimal place value from Modules 1 and 2, confirming that like units can be composed and decomposed—for example:

5 tenths + 7 tenths = 12 tenths = 1 and 2 tenths

5 eighths + 7 eighths = 12 eighths = 1 and 4 eighths

In Topic B, students move forward to see that fraction addition and subtraction are analogous to whole number addition and subtraction. Students add and subtract fractions with unlike denominators (5.NF.1) by replacing different fractional units with an equivalent fraction or like unit—for example:

1 fourth + 2 thirds = 3 twelfths + 8 twelfths = 11 twelfths

$$\frac{1}{4} + \frac{2}{3} = \frac{3}{12} + \frac{8}{12} = \frac{11}{12}$$

This is not a new concept but certainly a new level of complexity. Students have added equivalent or like units since kindergarten, adding frogs to frogs, ones to ones, tens to tens, and so on—for example:

1 boy + 2 girls = 1 child + 2 children = 3 children

1 liter − 375 mL = 1,000 mL − 375 mL = 625 mL

Throughout the module, a concrete to pictorial to abstract approach is used to convey this simple concept. Topic A uses paper strips and number line diagrams to clearly show equivalence. After a brief concrete introduction with folding paper, Topic B primarily uses the rectangular fractional model because it is useful for creating smaller like units via partitioning (e.g., thirds and fourths are changed to twelfths to create equivalent fractions, as in the diagram below). In Topic C, students move away from the pictorial altogether as they are empowered to write equations clarified by the model—for example:

$$\frac{1}{4} + \frac{2}{3} = \left(\frac{1 \times 3}{4 \times 3}\right) + \left(\frac{2 \times 4}{3 \times 4}\right) = \frac{3}{12} + \frac{8}{12} = \frac{11}{12}$$

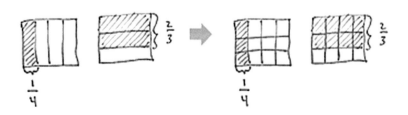

Topic C also uses the number line when adding and subtracting fractions greater than or equal to 1 so that students begin to see and manipulate fractions in relation to larger whole numbers and to each other. The number line takes fractions into the larger set of whole numbers—for example, "Between what two whole numbers will the sum of $1\frac{3}{4}$ and $5\frac{3}{5}$ lie?"

This leads to understanding of and skill with solving more interesting problems, often embedded within multistep word problems—for example:

Cristina and Matt's goal is to collect a total of $3\frac{1}{2}$ gallons of sap from the maple trees. Cristina collected $1\frac{3}{4}$ gallons. Matt collected $5\frac{3}{5}$ gallons. By how much did they beat their goal?

$$1\frac{3}{4}\text{ gal}+5\frac{3}{5}\text{ gal}-3\frac{1}{2}\text{ gal}=3+\left(\frac{3\times5}{4\times5}\right)+\left(\frac{3\times4}{5\times4}\right)-\left(\frac{1\times10}{2\times10}\right)$$

$$=3+\frac{15}{20}+\frac{12}{20}-\frac{10}{20}=3\frac{17}{20}\text{ gal}$$

Cristina and Matt beat their goal by $3\frac{17}{20}$ gallons.

Word problems are part of every lesson. Students are encouraged to draw bar diagrams, which allow analysis of the same part-whole relationships they have worked with since Grade 1.

In Topic D, students strategize to solve multiterm problems and more intensely assess the reasonableness of their solutions to word problems and their answers to fraction equations (5.NF.2)—for example, "I know my answer makes sense because the total amount of sap they collected is going to be about $7\frac{1}{2}$ gallons. Then, when we subtract 3 gallons, that is about $4\frac{1}{2}$. Then, $\frac{1}{2}$ less than that is about 4; $3\frac{17}{20}$ is just a little less than 4."

The Mid-Module Assessment follows Topic B. The End-of-Module Assessment follows Topic D.

FOCUS GRADE-LEVEL STANDARDS

Use equivalent fractions as a strategy to add and subtract fractions.[5]

5.NF.1 Add and subtract fractions with unlike denominators (including mixed numbers) by replacing given fractions with equivalent fractions in such a way as to produce an equivalent sum or difference of fractions with like denominators. For example, 2/3 + 5/4 = 8/12 + 15/12 = 23/12. (In general, a/b + c/d = (ad + bc)/bd.)

5.NF.2 Solve word problems involving addition and subtraction of fractions referring to the same whole, including cases of unlike denominators, e.g., by using visual fraction models or equations to represent the problem. Use benchmark fractions and number sense of fractions to estimate mentally and assess the reasonableness of answers. *For example, recognize an incorrect result 2/5 + 1/2 = 3/7, by observing that 3/7 < 1/2.*

FOUNDATIONAL STANDARDS

4.NF.1 Explain why a fraction a/b is equivalent to a fraction $(n \times a)/(n \times b)$ by using visual fraction models, with attention to how the number and size of the parts differ even though the two fractions themselves are the same size. Use this principle to recognize and generate equivalent fractions.

4.NF.3 Understand a fraction a/b with $a > 1$ as a sum of fractions $1/b$.

a. Understand addition and subtraction of fractions as joining and separating parts referring to the same whole.

b. Decompose a fraction into a sum of fractions with the same denominator in more than one way, recording each decomposition by an equation. Justify decompositions, e.g., by using a visual fraction model. *Examples: 3/8 = 1/8 + 1/8 + 1/8; 3/8 = 1/8 + 2/8; 2 1/8 = 1 + 1 + 1/8 = 8/8 + 8/8 + 1/8.*

c. Add and subtract mixed numbers with like denominators, e.g., by replacing each mixed number with an equivalent fraction, and/or by using properties of operations and the relationship between addition and subtraction.

d. Solve word problems involving addition and subtraction of fractions referring to the same whole and having like denominators, e.g., by using visual fraction models and equations to represent the problem.

FOCUS STANDARDS FOR MATHEMATICAL PRACTICE

MP.2 *Reason abstractly and quantitatively.* Mathematically proficient students make sense of quantities and their relationships in problem situations. They bring two complementary abilities to bear on problems involving quantitative relationships: the ability to *decontextualize*—to abstract a given situation and represent it symbolically and manipulate the representing symbols as if they have a life of their own, without necessarily attending to their referents—and the ability to *contextualize*—to pause as needed during the manipulation process in order to probe into the referents for the symbols involved. Quantitative reasoning entails habits of creating a coherent representation of the problem at hand; considering the units involved; attending to the meaning of quantities, not just how to compute them; and knowing and flexibly using different properties of operations and objects.

MP.3 *Construct viable arguments and critique the reasoning of others.* Mathematically proficient students understand and use stated assumptions, definitions, and previously established results in constructing arguments. They make conjectures and build a logical progression of statements to explore the truth of their conjectures. They are able to analyze situations by breaking them into cases and can recognize and use counterexamples. They justify their conclusions, communicate them to others, and respond to the arguments of others. They reason inductively about data, making plausible arguments that take into account the context from which the data arose. Mathematically proficient students are also able to compare the effectiveness of two plausible arguments, distinguish correct logic or reasoning from that which is flawed, and—if there is a flaw in argument—explain what it is.

Elementary students can construct arguments using concrete referents such as objects, drawings, diagrams, and actions. Such arguments can make sense and be correct, even though they are not generalized or made formal until later grades. Later, students learn to determine domains to which an argument applies. Students at all grade levels can listen to or read the arguments of others, decide whether they make sense, and ask useful questions to clarify or improve the arguments.

MP.4 *Model with mathematics.* Mathematically proficient students can apply the mathematics they know to solve problems arising in everyday life, society, and the workplace. In early grades, this might be as simple as writing an addition equation to describe a situation. In middle grades, a student might apply proportional reasoning to plan a school event or analyze a problem in the community. By high school, a student might use geometry to solve a design problem or use a function to describe how one quantity of interest depends on another. Mathematically proficient students who can apply what they know are comfortable making assumptions and approximations to simplify a complicated situation, realizing that these may need revision later. They are able to identify important quantities in a practical situation and map their relationships using such tools as diagrams, two-way tables, graphs, flowcharts, and formulas. They can analyze those relationships mathematically to draw conclusions. They routinely interpret their mathematical results in the context of the situation and reflect on whether the results make sense, possibly improving the model if it has not served its purpose.

MP.5 *Use appropriate tools strategically.* Mathematically proficient students consider the available tools when solving a mathematical problem. These tools might include pencil and paper, concrete models, a ruler, a protractor, a calculator, a spreadsheet, a computer algebra system, a statistical package, or dynamic geometry software. Proficient students are sufficiently familiar with tools appropriate for their grade or course to make sound decisions about when each of these tools might be helpful, recognizing both the insight to be gained and their limitations. For example, mathematically proficient high school students analyze graphs of functions and solutions generated using a graphing calculator. They detect possible errors by strategically using estimation and other mathematical knowledge. When making mathematical models, they know that technology can enable them to visualize the results of varying assumptions, explore consequences, and compare predictions with data. Mathematically proficient students at various grade levels are able to identify relevant external mathematical resources, such as digital content located on a website, and use them to pose or solve problems. They are able to use technological tools to explore and deepen their understanding of concepts.

MP.6 *Attend to precision.* Mathematically proficient students try to communicate precisely to others. They try to use clear definitions in discussion with others and in their own reasoning. They state the meaning of the symbols they choose, including using the equal sign consistently and appropriately. They are careful about specifying units of measure and labeling axes to clarify the correspondence with quantities in a problem. They calculate accurately and efficiently, expressing numerical answers with a degree of precision appropriate for the problem context. In the elementary grades, students give carefully formulated explanations to each other. By the time they reach high school, they have learned to examine claims and make explicit use of definitions.

MP.7 *Look for and make use of structure.* Mathematically proficient students look closely to discern a pattern or structure. Young students, for example, might notice that 3 and 7 more is the same amount as 7 and 3 more, or they may sort a collection of shapes according to how many sides the shapes have. Later, students will see 7 × 8 equals the well-remembered 7 × 5 + 7 × 3, in preparation for learning about the distributive property. In the expression $x^2 + 9x + 14$, older students can see the 14 as 2 × 7 and the 9 as 2 + 7. They recognize the significance of an existing line in a geometric figure and can use the strategy of drawing an auxiliary line for solving problems. They also can step back for an overview and shift perspective. They can see complicated things, such as some algebraic expressions, as single objects or as being composed of several objects. For example, they can see $5 - 3(x - y)^2$ as 5 minus a positive number times a square and use that to realize that its value cannot be more than 5 for any real numbers x and y.

MODULE TOPIC SUMMARIES

Topic A: Equivalent Fractions

In Topic A, students revisit the foundational Grade 4 standards addressing equivalence. When equivalent, fractions can be represented by the same amount of area of a rectangle and by the same point on a number line. Areas are subdivided. Lengths on the number line are divided into smaller equal lengths. On the number line below, there are 4 × 3 parts of equal length. From both the area model and the number line, it can be seen that 2 thirds is equivalent to 8 twelfths.

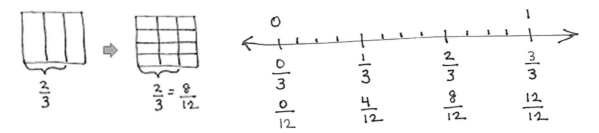

This equivalence can also be represented symbolically.

$$\frac{2}{3} = \frac{2 \times 4}{3 \times 4} = \frac{8}{12}$$

Furthermore, equivalence is evidenced when adding fractions with the same denominator. The sum may be decomposed into parts (or recomposed into an equal sum)—for example:

$$\frac{2}{3} = \frac{1}{3} + \frac{1}{3}$$

$$\frac{7}{8} = \frac{3}{8} + \frac{3}{8} + \frac{1}{8}$$

$$\frac{6}{2} = \frac{2}{2} + \frac{2}{2} + \frac{2}{2} = 1 + 1 + 1 = 3$$

$$\frac{8}{5} = \frac{5}{5} + \frac{3}{5} = 1\frac{3}{5}$$

$$\frac{7}{3} = \frac{6}{3} + \frac{1}{3} = 2 \times \frac{3}{3} + \frac{1}{3} = 2 + \frac{1}{3} = 2\frac{1}{3}$$

In Lesson 1, students analyze what is happening to the units when an equivalent fraction is being made by changing larger units for smaller ones, honing their ability to look for and make use of structure (MP.7). They study the area model to make generalizations, transferring that back onto the number line as they see the same process occurring there within the lengths.

Focus Standard:	4.NF.1	Explain why a fraction a/b is equivalent to a fraction (n x a)/(n x b) by using visual fraction models, with attention to how the number and size of the parts differ even though the two fractions themselves are the same size. Use this principle to recognize and generate equivalent fractions.
Instructional Days:	2	
Coherence		
Links from:	G4–M5	Fraction Equivalence, Ordering, and Operations
Links to:	G5–M4	Multiplication and Division of Fractions and Decimal Fractions
	G6–M3	Rational Numbers

Objective 1: Make equivalent fractions with the number line, the area model, and numbers. (Lesson 1)

Objective 2: Make equivalent fractions with sums of fractions with like denominators. (Lesson 2)

Topic B: Making Like Units Pictorially

In Module 3, students use the familiar rectangular fraction model to add and subtract fractions with unlike denominators.

Students make like units with all addends or both minuend and subtrahend. First, they draw a wide rectangle and partition it with vertical lines as they would a bar diagram (also known as tape diagram), representing the first fraction with a bracket and shading. They then partition a second congruent rectangle with horizontal lines to show the second fraction. Next, they partition both rectangles with matching lines to create like units.

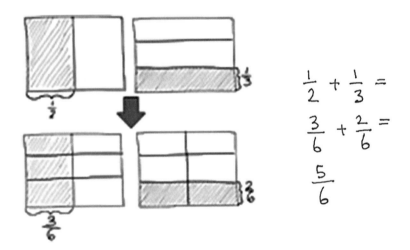

$$\frac{1}{2} + \frac{1}{3} =$$

$$\frac{3}{6} + \frac{2}{6} =$$

$$\frac{5}{6}$$

This method requires that they see 3 units as equal to 1 half and 2 units as equal to 1 third. They practice making these models extensively until they internalize the process of making like units. Students use the same systematic drawing for addition and subtraction. In this manner, they are prepared to generalize with understanding to multiply the numerator and denominator by the same number. The topic closes with a lesson devoted to solving two-step word problems.

Focus Standard:	5.NF.1	Add and subtract fractions with unlike denominators (including mixed numbers) by replacing given fractions with equivalent fractions in such a way as to produce an equivalent sum or difference of fractions with like denominators. *For example, 2/3 + 5/4 = 8/12 + 15/12 = 23/12. (In general, a/b + c/d = (ad + bc)/bd.).*
	5.NF.2	Solve word problems involving addition and subtraction of fractions referring to the same whole, including cases of unlike denominators, e.g., by using visual fraction models or equations to represent the problem. Use benchmark fractions and number sense of fractions to estimate mentally and assess the reasonableness of answers. *For example, recognize an incorrect result 2/5 + 1/2 = 3/7, by observing that 3/7 < 1/2*
Instructional Days:	5	
Coherence		
Links from:	G4–M5	Fraction Equivalence, Ordering, and Operations
Links to:	G5–M4	Multiplication and Division of Fractions and Decimal Fractions
	G6–M3	Rational Numbers

Objective 1: Add fractions with unlike units using the strategy of creating equivalent fractions.
(Lesson 3)

Objective 2: Add fractions with sums between 1 and 2.
(Lesson 4)

Objective 3: Subtract fractions with unlike units using the strategy of creating equivalent fractions.
(Lesson 5)

Objective 4: Subtract fractions from numbers between 1 and 2.
(Lesson 6)

Objective 5: Solve two-step word problems.
(Lesson 7)

Topic C: Making Like Units Numerically

Topic C uses the number line when adding and subtracting fractions greater than or equal to 1. The number line helps students see that fractions are analogous to whole numbers. The number line makes it clear that numbers on the left are smaller than numbers on the right (which helps lead to integers in Grade 6). Using this tool, students recognize and manipulate fractions in relation to larger whole numbers and to each other—for example, "Between what two whole numbers does the sum of $1\frac{2}{3}$ and $5\frac{3}{4}$ lie?"

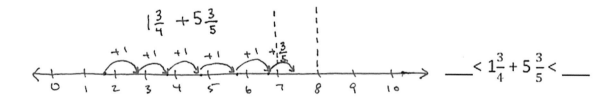

This leads to understanding of and skill with solving more interesting problems, often embedded within multistep word problems:

Cristina and Matt's goal is to collect a total of $3\frac{1}{2}$ gallons of sap from the maple trees. Cristina collected $1\frac{3}{4}$ gallons. Matt collected $5\frac{3}{5}$ gallons. By how much did they beat their goal?

$$1\frac{3}{4}\,gal + 5\frac{3}{5}\,gal - 3\frac{1}{2}\,gal = 3 + \left(\frac{3\times5}{4\times5}\right) + \left(\frac{3\times4}{5\times4}\right) - \left(\frac{1\times10}{2\times10}\right)$$

$$= 3 + \frac{15}{20} + \frac{12}{20} - \frac{10}{20} = 3\frac{17}{20}\,gal$$

Cristina and Matt beat their goal by $3\frac{17}{20}$ gallons.

Word problems are part of every lesson. Students are encouraged to use bar diagrams, which facilitate analysis of the same part-whole relationships they have worked with since Grade 1.

Focus Standard:	5.NF.1	Add and subtract fractions with unlike denominators (including mixed numbers) by replacing given fractions with equivalent fractions in such a way as to produce an equivalent sum or difference of fractions with like denominators. *For example, 2/3 + 5/4 = 8/12 + 15/12 = 23/12. (In general, a/b + c/d = (ad + bc)/bd.).*
	5.NF.2	Solve word problems involving addition and subtraction of fractions referring to the same whole, including cases of unlike denominators, e.g., by using visual fraction models or equations to represent the problem. Use benchmark fractions and number sense of fractions to estimate mentally and assess the reasonableness of answers. *For example, recognize an incorrect result 2/5 + 1/2 = 3/7, by observing that 3/7 < 1/2*
Instructional Days:	5	
Coherence		
Links from:	G4–M5	Fraction Equivalence, Ordering, and Operations
	G5–M1	Place Value and Decimal Fractions
Links to:	G5–M4	Multiplication and Division of Fractions and Decimal Fractions

Objective 1: Add fractions to and subtract fractions from whole numbers using equivalence and the number line as strategies.
(Lesson 8)

Objective 2: Add fractions making like units numerically.
(Lesson 9)

Objective 3: Add fractions with sums greater than 2.
(Lesson 10)

Objective 4: Subtract fractions making like units numerically.
(Lesson 11)

Objective 5: Subtract fractions greater than or equal to 1.
(Lesson 12)

Topic D: Further Applications

Topic D opens with students estimating the value of expressions involving sums and differences with fractions. "Is your sum less than or greater than 1 half? One? How do you know?" Though these conversations have been embedded within almost every debriefing up to this point, by setting aside an instructional day to dig deeply into logical arguments, students see that it is very easy to forget to make sense of numbers when calculating. This is really the theme of this topic: reasoning while using fractions.

Lesson 14 encourages students to look for relationships before calculating, for example, to use the tool of the associative property or what they know about parts and wholes. Looking for relationships allows them to see shortcuts and connections that are so often bypassed in the rush to get the answer.

In Lesson 15, students solve multistep word problems and actively assess the reasonableness of their answers. In Lesson 16, they explore part-to-whole relationships while solving a challenging problem: "One half of Nell's money is equal to two thirds of Jennifer's." This lesson challenges the underlying assumption of all fraction arithmetic: that when adding and subtracting, fractions are always defined in relationship to the same whole amount. The beauty of this exploration is to see students grasp that one half of one thing can be equivalent to two thirds of another.

Focus Standard:	5.NF.1	Add and subtract fractions with unlike denominators (including mixed numbers) by replacing given fractions with equivalent fractions in such a way as to produce an equivalent sum or difference of fractions with like denominators. *For example, 2/3 + 5/4 = 8/12 + 15/12 = 23/12. (In general, a/b + c/d = (ad + bc)/bd.).*
	5.NF.2	Solve word problems involving addition and subtraction of fractions referring to the same whole, including cases of unlike denominators, e.g., by using visual fraction models or equations to represent the problem. Use benchmark fractions and number sense of fractions to estimate mentally and assess the reasonableness of answers. *For example, recognize an incorrect result 2/5 + 1/2 = 3/7, by observing that 3/7 < 1/2.*
Instructional Days:	4	
Coherence Links from:	G4–M5	Fraction Equivalence, Ordering, and Operations
	G5–M1	Place Value and Decimal Fractions
Links to:	G5–M4	Multiplication and Division of Fractions and Decimal Fractions

Objective 1: Use fraction benchmark numbers to assess the reasonableness of addition and subtraction equations.
(Lesson 13)

Objective 2: Strategize to solve multiterm problems.
(Lesson 14)

Objective 3: Solve multistep word problems; assess the reasonableness of solutions using benchmark numbers.
(Lesson 15)

Objective 4: Explore part-to-whole relationships.
(Lesson 16)

MODULE 4: MULTIPLICATION AND DIVISION OF FRACTIONS AND DECIMAL FRACTIONS

OVERVIEW

In Module 4, students learn to multiply fractions and decimal fractions and begin work with fraction division.

Topic A begins the 38-day module with an exploration of fractional measurement. Students construct line plots by measuring the same objects using three different rulers accurate to $\frac{1}{2}$, $\frac{1}{4}$, and $\frac{1}{8}$ of an inch (5.MD.2).

Students compare the line plots and explain how changing the accuracy of the unit of measure affects the distribution of points. This is foundational to the understanding that measurement is inherently imprecise, as it is limited by the accuracy of the tool at hand. Students use their knowledge of fraction operations to explore questions that arise from the plotted data. The interpretation of a fraction as division is inherent in this exploration. To measure to the quarter inch, 1 inch must be divided into four equal parts, or $1 \div 4$. This reminder of the meaning of a fraction as a point on a number line, coupled with the embedded, informal exploration of fractions as division, provides a bridge to Topic B's more formal treatment of fractions as division.

Interpreting fractions as division is the focus of Topic B. Equal sharing with area models (both concrete and pictorial) gives students an opportunity to make sense of division of whole numbers with answers in the form of fractions or mixed numbers (e.g., seven brownies shared by three girls; three pizzas shared by four people). Discussion also includes an interpretation of remainders as a fraction (5.NF.3). Tape diagrams provide a linear model of these problems. Moreover, students see that by renaming larger units in terms of smaller units, division resulting in a fraction is just like whole number division.

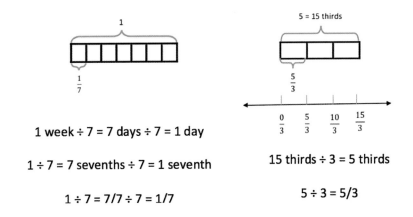

1 week ÷ 7 = 7 days ÷ 7 = 1 day

1 ÷ 7 = 7 sevenths ÷ 7 = 1 seventh

1 ÷ 7 = 7/7 ÷ 7 = 1/7

15 thirds ÷ 3 = 5 thirds

5 ÷ 3 = 5/3

Topic B continues as students solve real-world problems (5.NF.3) and generate story contexts for visual models. The topic concludes with students making connections between models and equations while reasoning about their results (e.g., "Between what two whole numbers does the answer lie?").

In Topic C, students interpret finding a fraction of a set ($\frac{3}{4}$ of 24) as multiplication of a whole number by a fraction ($\frac{3}{4} \times 24$) and use tape diagrams to support their understandings (5.NF.4a). This in turn leads students to see division by a whole number as equivalent to multiplication by its reciprocal. That is, division by 2, for example, is the same as multiplication by $\frac{1}{2}$. Students also use the commutative property to relate fraction of a set to the Grade 4 repeated addition interpretation of multiplication by a fraction. This opens the door for students to reason about various strategies for multiplying fractions and whole numbers. Students apply their knowledge of fraction of a set and previous conversion experiences (with scaffolding from a conversion chart, if necessary) to find a fraction of a measurement, thus converting a larger unit to an equivalent smaller unit (e.g., $\frac{1}{3}$ minutes = 20 seconds and $2\frac{1}{4}$ feet = 27 inches).

Interpreting numerical expressions opens Topic D as students learn to evaluate expressions with parentheses, such as $3 \times (\frac{2}{3} - \frac{1}{5})$ or $\frac{2}{3} \times (7 + 9)$ (5.OA.1). They then learn to interpret numerical expressions such as 3 *times the difference between* $\frac{2}{3}$ *and* $\frac{1}{5}$ or *two-thirds the sum of 7 and 9* (5.OA.2). Students generate word problems that lead to the same calculation (5.NF.4a), such as, "Kelly combined 7 ounces of carrot juice and 5 ounces of orange juice in a glass. Jack drank $\frac{2}{3}$ of the mixture. How much did Jack drink?" Solving word problems (5.NF.6) allows students to apply new knowledge of fraction multiplication in context, and tape diagrams are used to model multistep problems requiring the use of addition, subtraction, and multiplication of fractions.

Topic E introduces students to multiplication of fractions by fractions—in both fraction and decimal form (5.NF.4a, 5.NBT.7). The topic starts with multiplying a unit fraction by a unit fraction and progresses to multiplying two nonunit fractions. Students use area models, rectangular arrays, and tape diagrams to model the multiplication. These familiar models help students draw parallels between whole number and fraction multiplication and solve word problems. This intensive work with fractions positions students to extend their previous work with decimal-by-whole number multiplication to decimal-by-decimal multiplication. Just as students used unit form to multiply fractional units by wholes in Module 2 (e.g., 3.5 × 2 = 35 tenths × 2 ones = 70 tenths), they will connect fraction-by-fraction multiplication to multiply fractional units by fractional units (3.5 × 0.2 = 35 tenths × 2 tenths = 70 hundredths).

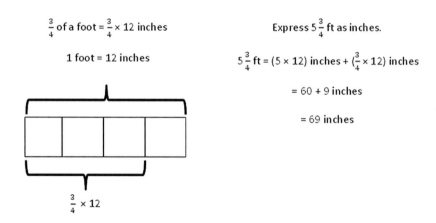

Reasoning about decimal placement is an integral part of these lessons. Finding fractional parts of customary measurements and measurement conversion (5.MD.1) concludes Topic E. Students convert smaller units to fractions of a larger unit (e.g., 6 inches = $\frac{1}{2}$ feet). The inclusion of customary units provides a meaningful context for many common fractions (e.g., $\frac{1}{2}$ pint = 1 cup, $\frac{1}{3}$ yard = 1 foot, $\frac{1}{4}$ gallon = 1 quart). This topic, together with the fraction concepts and skills learned in Module 3, opens the door to a wide variety of application word problems (5.NF.6).

Students interpret multiplication in Grade 3 as equal groups, and in Grade 4 students begin to understand multiplication as comparison. Here, in Topic F, students once again extend their understanding of multiplication to include scaling (5.NF.5). Students compare the product to the size of one factor, given the size of the other factor (5.NF.5a), without calculation (e.g., 486 × 1,327.45 is twice as large as 243 × 1,327.45, because 486 = 2 × 243). This reasoning, along with the other work of this module, sets the stage for students to reason about the size of products when quantities are multiplied by numbers larger than 1 and smaller than 1. Students relate their previous work with equivalent fractions to interpreting multiplication by $\frac{n}{n}$ as multiplication by 1 (5.NF.5b). Students build on their new understanding of fraction equivalence as multiplication by $\frac{n}{n}$ to convert fractions to decimals and decimals to fractions. For example, $\frac{3}{25}$ is easily renamed in hundredths as $\frac{12}{100}$ using multiplication of $\frac{4}{4}$. The word form of *twelve hundredths* will then be used to notate this quantity as a decimal. Conversions between fractional forms will be limited to fractions whose denominators are factors of 10, 100, or 1,000. Students will apply the concepts of the topic to real-world, multistep problems (5.NF.6).

Topic G begins the work of division with fractions, both fractions and decimal fractions. Students use tape diagrams and number lines to reason about the division of a whole number by a unit fraction and a unit fraction by a whole number (5.NF.7). Using the same thinking developed in Module 2 to divide whole numbers, students reason about how many fourths are in 5 when considering such cases as $5 \div \frac{1}{4}$. They also reason about the size of the unit when $\frac{1}{4}$ is partitioned into 5 equal parts: $\frac{1}{4} \div 5$. Using this thinking as a backdrop, students are introduced to decimal fraction divisors and use equivalent fraction and place value thinking to reason about the size of quotients, calculate quotients, and sensibly place the decimal in quotients (5.NBT.7).

The module concludes with Topic H, in which numerical expressions involving fraction-by-fraction multiplication are interpreted and evaluated (5.OA.1, 5.OA.2). Students create and solve word problems involving both multiplication and division of fractions and decimal fractions.

The Mid-Module Assessment is administered after Topic D, and the End-of-Module Assessment follows Topic H.

FOCUS GRADE-LEVEL STANDARDS

Write and interpret numerical expressions.

5.OA.1 Use parentheses, brackets, or braces in numerical expressions, and evaluate expressions with these symbols.

5.OA.2 Write simple expressions that record calculations with numbers, and interpret numerical expressions without evaluating them. *For example, express the calculation "add 8 and 7, then multiply by 2" as 2 × (8 + 7). Recognize that 3 × (18,932 + 921) is three times as large as 18,932 + 921, without having to calculate the indicated sum or product.*

Perform operations with multi-digit whole numbers and with decimals to hundredths.

5.NBT.7 Add, subtract, multiply, and divide decimals to hundredths, using concrete models or drawings and strategies based on place value, properties of operations, and/or the relationship between addition and subtraction; relate the strategy to a written method and explain the reasoning used.

Apply and extend previous understandings of multiplication and division to multiply and divide fractions.

5.NF.3 Interpret a fraction as division of the numerator by the denominator ($a/b = a : b$). Solve word problems involving division of whole numbers leading to answers in the form of fractions or mixed numbers, e.g., by using visual fraction models or equations to represent the problem. *For example, interpret 3/4 as the result of dividing 3 by 4, noting that 3/4 multiplied by 4 equals 3, and that when 3 wholes are shared equally among 4 people each person has a share of size 3/4. If 9 people want to share a 50-pound sack of rice equally by weight, how many pounds of rice should each person get? Between what two whole numbers does your answer lie?*

5.NF.4 Apply and extend previous understandings of multiplication to multiply a fraction or whole number by a fraction.

    a.   Interpret the product of $(a/b) \times q$ as a parts of a partition of q into b equal parts; equivalently, as the result of a sequence of operations $a \times q \div b$. *For example, use a visual fraction model to show* $(2/3) \times 4 = 8/3$*, and create a story context for this equation. Do the same with* $(2/3) \times (4/5) = 8/15$*. (In general,* $(a/b) \times (c/d) = ac/bd$*.)*

5.NF.5 Interpret multiplication as scaling (resizing), by:

    a.   Comparing the size of a product to the size of one factor on the basis of the size of the other factor, without performing the indicated multiplication.

    b.   Explaining why multiplying a given number by a fraction greater than 1 results in a product greater than the given number (recognizing multiplication by whole numbers greater than 1 as a familiar case); explaining why multiplying a given number by a fraction less than 1 results in a product smaller than the given number; and relating the principle of fraction equivalence $a/b = (n \times a)/(n \times b)$ to the effect of multiplying a/b by 1.

5.NF.6 Solve real world problems involving multiplication of fractions and mixed numbers, e.g., by using visual fraction models or equations to represent the problem.

5.NF.7 Apply and extend previous understandings of division to divide unit fractions by whole numbers and whole numbers by unit fractions. (Students able to multiply fractions in general can develop strategies to divide fractions in general, by reasoning about the relationship between multiplication and division. But division of a fraction by a fraction is not a requirement at this grade level.)

    a.   Interpret division of a unit fraction by a non-zero whole number, and compute such quotients. *For example, create a story context for* $(1/3) \div 4$*, and use a visual fraction model to show the quotient. Use the relationship between multiplication and division to explain that* $(1/3) \div 4 = 1/12$ *because* $(1/12) \times 4 = 1/3$*.*

    b.   Interpret division of a whole number by a unit fraction, and compute such quotients. *For example, create a story context for* $4 \div (1/5)$*, and use a visual fraction model to show the quotient. Use the relationship between multiplication and division to explain that* $4 \div (1/5) = 20$ *because* $20 \times (1/5) = 4$*.*

    c.   Solve real world problems involving division of unit fractions by non-zero whole numbers and division of whole numbers by unit fractions, e.g., by using visual fraction models and equations to represent the problem. *For example, how much chocolate will each person get if 3 people share 1/2 lb of chocolate equally? How many 1/3-cup servings are in 2 cups of raisins?*

Convert like measurement units within a given measurement system.

5.MD.1 Convert among different-sized standard measurement units within a given measurement system (e.g., convert 5 cm to 0.05 m), and use these conversions in solving multistep, real world problems.

Represent and interpret data.

5.MD.2 Make a line plot to display a data set of measurements in fractions of a unit (1/2, 1/4, 1/8). Use operations on fractions for this grade to solve problems involving information presented in line plots. *For example, given different measurements of liquid in identical beakers, find the amount of liquid each beaker would contain if the total amount in all the beakers were redistributed equally.*

FOUNDATIONAL STANDARDS

4.NF.1 Explain why a fraction a/b is equivalent to a fraction $(n \times a)/(n \times b)$ by using visual fraction models, with attention to how the number and size of the parts differ even though the two fractions themselves are the same size. Use this principle to recognize and generate equivalent fractions.

4.NF.2 Compare two fractions with different numerators and different denominators, e.g., by creating common denominators or numerators, or by comparing to a benchmark fraction such as 1/2. Recognize that comparisons are valid only when the two fractions refer to the same whole. Record the results of comparisons with symbols >, =, or <, and justify the conclusions, e.g., by using a visual fraction model.

4.NF.3 Understand a fraction a/b with $a > 1$ as a sum of fractions $1/b$.

  a. Understand addition and subtraction of fractions as joining and separating parts referring to the same whole.

  b. Decompose a fraction into a sum of fractions with the same denominator in more than one way, recording each decomposition by an equation. Justify decompositions, e.g., by using a visual fraction model. *Examples: 3/8 = 1/8 + 1/8 + 1/8; 3/8 = 1/8 + 2/8; 2 1/8 = 1 + 1 + 1/8 = 8/8 + 8/8 + 1/8.*

4.NF.4 Apply and extend previous understandings of multiplication to multiply a fraction by a whole number.

  a. Understand a fraction a/b as a multiple of $1/b$. *For example, use a visual fraction model to represent 5/4 as the product 5 × (1/4), recording the conclusion by the equation 5/4 = 5 × (1/4).*

  b. Understand a multiple of a/b as a multiple of $1/b$, and use this understanding to multiply a fraction by a whole number. *For example, use a visual fraction model to express 3 × (2/5) as 6 × (1/5), recognizing this product as 6/5. (In general, n × (a/b) = (n × a)/b.)*

  c. Solve word problems involving multiplication of a fraction by a whole number, e.g., by using visual fraction models and equations to represent the problem. *For example, if each person at a party will eat 3/8 of a pound of roast beef and there will be 5 people at the party, how many pounds of roast beef will be needed? Between what two whole numbers does your answer lie?*

4.NF.5 Express a fraction with denominator 10 as an equivalent fraction with denominator 100, and use this technique to add two fractions with respective denominators 10 and 100. (Students who can generate equivalent fractions can develop strategies for adding fractions with unlike denominators in general. But addition and subtraction with unlike denominators in general is not a requirement at this grade.) *For example, express 3/10 as 30/100, and add 3/10 + 4/100 = 34/100.*

4.NF.6 Use decimal notation for fractions with denominators 10 or 100. *For example, rewrite 0.62 as 62/100; describe a length as 0.62 meters; locate 0.62 on a number line diagram.*

FOCUS STANDARDS FOR MATHEMATICAL PRACTICE

MP.2 *Reason abstractly and quantitatively.* Students reason abstractly and quantitatively as they interpret the size of a product in relation to the size of a factor, interpret terms in a multiplication sentence as a quantity and a scaling factor, and then create a coherent representation of the problem at hand while attending to the meaning of the quantities.

MP.4 *Model with mathematics.* Students model with mathematics as they solve word problems involving multiplication and division of fractions and decimals and identify important quantities in a practical situation and map their relationships using diagrams. Students use a line plot to model measurement data and interpret their results in the context of the situation, reflect on whether results make sense, and possibly improve the model if it has not served its purpose.

MP.5 *Use appropriate tools strategically.* Students use rulers to measure objects to the 1/2-, 1/4-, and 1/8-inch increments recognizing both the insight to be gained and the limitations of this tool as they learn that the actual object may not match the mathematical model precisely.

MODULE TOPIC SUMMARIES

Topic A: Line Plots of Fraction Measurements

Topic A begins the 38-day module with an exploration of fractional measurement. Students construct line plots by measuring the same objects using three different rulers accurate to $\frac{1}{2}$, $\frac{1}{4}$, and $\frac{1}{8}$ inch (5.MD.2). They compare the line plots and explain how changing the accuracy of the unit of measure affects the distribution of points (see line plots below). This is foundational to the understanding that measurement is inherently imprecise as it is limited by the accuracy of the tool at hand.

Students use their knowledge of fraction operations to explore questions that arise from the plotted data: "What is the total length of the five longest pencils in our class? Can the half-inch line plot be reconstructed using only data from the quarter-inch plot? Why or why not?" The interpretation of a fraction as division is inherent in this exploration. To measure to the quarter inch, 1 inch must be divided into 4 equal parts, or $1 \div 4$. This reminder of the meaning of a fraction as a point on a number line coupled with the embedded, informal exploration of fractions as division provides a bridge to Topic B's more formal treatment of fractions as division.

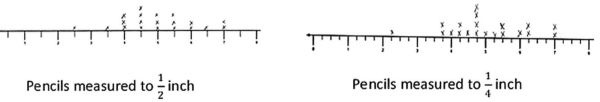

Pencils measured to $\frac{1}{2}$ inch   Pencils measured to $\frac{1}{4}$ inch

Focus Standard:	5.MD.2	Make a line plot to display a data set of measurements in fractions of a unit (1/2, 1/4, 1/8). Use operations on fractions for this grade to solve problems involving information presented in line plots. For example, given different measurements of liquid in identical beakers, find the amount of liquid each beaker would contain if the total amount in all the beakers were redistributed equally.
Instructional Days:	1	
Coherence		
Links from:	G4–M5	Fraction Equivalence, Ordering, and Operations
Links to:	G6–M2	Arithmetic Operations Including Dividing by a Fraction

Objective 1: Measure and compare pencil lengths to the nearest $\frac{1}{2}$, $\frac{1}{4}$, and $\frac{1}{8}$ of an inch, and analyze the data through line plots.
(Lesson 1)

Topic B: Fractions as Division

Interpreting fractions as division is the focus of Topic B. Equal sharing with area models (both concrete and pictorial) gives students an opportunity to make sense of the division of whole numbers with answers in the form of fractions or mixed numbers (e.g., seven brownies shared by three girls, three pizzas shared by four people). Discussion also includes an interpretation of remainders as a fraction (5.NF.3). Tape diagrams provide a linear model of these problems. Moreover, students see that by renaming larger units in terms of smaller units, division resulting in a fraction is just like whole number division.

Topic B continues as students solve real-world problems (5.NF.3) and generate story contexts for visual models. The topic concludes with students making connections between models and equations while reasoning about their results (e.g., between what two whole numbers does the answer lie?).

Focus Standard:	5.NF.3	Interpret a fraction as division of the numerator by the denominator ($a/b = a \div b$). Solve word problems involving division of whole numbers leading to answers in the form of fractions or mixed numbers, e.g., by using visual fraction models or equations to represent the problem. *For example, interpret 3/4 as the result of dividing 3 by 4, noting that 3/4 multiplied by 4 equals 3, and that when 3 wholes are shared equally among 4 people each person has a share of size 3/4. If 9 people want to share a 50-pound sack of rice equally by weight, how many pounds of rice should each person get? Between what two whole numbers does your answer lie?*
Instructional Days:	4	
Coherence		
Links from:	G4–M5	Fraction Equivalence, Ordering, and Operations
	G4–M6	Decimal Fractions
Links to:	G6–M2	Arithmetic Operations Including Dividing by a Fraction

Objective 1: Interpret a fraction as division.
(Lessons 2 and 3)

Objective 2: Use tape diagrams to model fractions as division.
(Lesson 4)

Objective 3: Solve word problems involving the division of whole numbers with answers in the form of fractions or whole numbers.
(Lesson 5)

Topic C: Multiplication of a Whole Number by a Fraction

In Topic C, students interpret finding a fraction of a set ($\frac{3}{4}$ of 24) as multiplication of a whole number by a fraction ($\frac{3}{4} \times 24$) and use tape diagrams to support their understandings (5.NF.4a). This in turn leads students to see division by a whole number as equivalent to multiplication by its reciprocal; that is, division by 2, for example, is the same as multiplication by $\frac{1}{2}$.

Students also use the commutative property to relate fraction of a set to the Grade 4 repeated addition interpretation of multiplication by a fraction. This opens the door for students to reason about various strategies for multiplying fractions and whole numbers. Students apply their knowledge of fraction of a set and previous conversion experiences (with scaffolding from a conversion chart, if necessary) to find a fraction of a measurement, thus converting a larger unit to an equivalent smaller unit (e.g., $\frac{1}{3}$ minutes = 20 seconds and $2\frac{1}{4}$ feet = 27 inches).

Focus Standard:	5.NF.4a	Apply and extend previous understandings of multiplication to multiply a fraction or whole number by a fraction.
		a. Interpret the product of *(a/b)* × *q* as *a* parts of a partition of *q* into *b* equal parts; equivalently, as the result of a sequence of operations *a* × *q* ÷ *b*. For example, use a visual fraction model to show *(2/3)* × *4* = *8/3*, and create a story context for this equation. Do the same with *(2/3)* × *(4/5)* = *8/15*. (In general, *(a/b)* × *(c/d)* = *ac/bd*.)
Instructional Days:	4	
Coherence		
Links from:	G4–M5	Fraction Equivalence, Ordering, and Operations
Links to:	G6–M2	Arithmetic Operations Including Dividing by a Fraction

Objective 1: Relate fractions as division to fraction of a set.
(Lesson 6)

Objective 2: Multiply any whole number by a fraction using tape diagrams.
(Lesson 7)

Objective 3: Relate fraction of a set to the repeated addition interpretation of fraction multiplication.
(Lesson 8)

Objective 4: Find a fraction of a measurement, and solve word problems.
(Lesson 9)

Topic D: Fraction Expressions and Word Problems

Interpreting numerical expressions opens Topic D as students learn to evaluate expressions with parentheses, such as $3 \times (\frac{2}{3} - 1/5)$ or $\frac{2}{3} \times (7 + 9)$ (5.OA.1). They then learn to interpret numerical expressions such as 3 *times the difference between* $\frac{2}{3}$ *and* $\frac{1}{5}$ or $\frac{2}{3}$ *the sum of 7 and 9* (5.OA.2). Students generate word problems that lead to the same calculation (5.NF.4a), such as, "Kelly combined 7 ounces of carrot juice and 5 ounces of orange juice in a glass. Jack drank $\frac{2}{3}$ of the mixture. How much did Jack drink?" Solving word problems (5.NF.6) allows students to apply new knowledge of fraction multiplication in context, and tape diagrams are used to model multistep problems requiring the use of addition, subtraction, and multiplication of fractions.

Focus Standard:	5.OA.1	Use parentheses, brackets, or braces in numerical expressions, and evaluate expressions with these symbols.
	5.OA.2	Write simple expressions that record calculations with numbers, and interpret numerical expressions without evaluating them. *For example, express the calculation "add 8 and 7, then multiply by 2" as 2 × (8 +7). Recognize that 3 × (18,932 + 921) is three times as large as 18,932 + 921, without having to calculate the indicated sum or product.*
	5.NF.4a	Apply and extend previous understandings of multiplication to multiply a fraction or whole number by a fraction.
		a. Interpret the product of (a/b) × q as a parts of a partition of q into b equal parts; equivalently, as the result of a sequence of operations a × q ÷ b. *For example, use a visual fraction model to show (2/3) × 4 = 8/3, and create a story context for this equation. Do the same with (2/3) × (4/5) = 8/15. (In general, (a/b) × (c/d) = ac/bd.)*
	5.NF.6	Solve real world problems involving multiplication of fractions and mixed numbers, e.g., by using visual fraction models or equations to represent the problem.
Instructional Days:	3	
Coherence		
Links from:	G4–M2	Unit Conversions and Problem Solving with Metric Measurement
Links to:	G6–M2	Arithmetic Operations Including Dividing by a Fraction

Objective 1: Compare and evaluate expressions with parentheses.
(Lesson 10)

Objective 2: Solve and create fraction word problems involving addition, subtraction, and multiplication.
(Lessons 11 and 12)

Topic E: Multiplication of a Fraction by a Fraction

Topic E introduces students to multiplication of fractions by fractions—in both fraction and decimal form (5.NF.4a, 5.NBT.7). The topic starts with multiplying a unit fraction by a unit fraction and progresses to multiplying two nonunit fractions. Students use area models, rectangular arrays, and tape diagrams to model the multiplication. These familiar models help students draw parallels between whole number and fraction multiplication and solve word problems. This intensive work with fractions positions students to extend their previous work with decimal-by-whole number multiplication to decimal-by-decimal multiplication. Just as students used unit form to multiply fractional units by wholes in Module 2 (e.g., 3.5 × 2 = 35 tenths × 2 ones = 70 tenths), they will connect fraction-by-fraction multiplication to multiply fractional units by fractional units (3.5 × 0.2 = 35 tenths × 2 tenths = 70 hundredths).

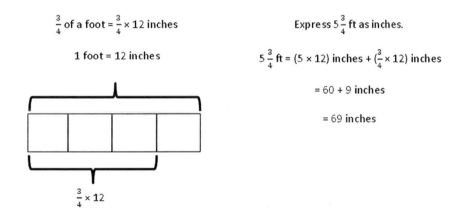

Reasoning about decimal placement is an integral part of these lessons. Finding fractional parts of customary measurements and measurement conversion (5.MD.1) concludes Topic E. Students convert smaller units to fractions of a larger unit (e.g., 6 inches = $\frac{1}{2}$ foot). The inclusion of customary units provides a meaningful context for many common fractions (e.g., $\frac{1}{2}$ pint = 1 cup, $\frac{1}{3}$ yard = 1 foot, $\frac{1}{4}$ gallon = 1 quart). This topic, together with the fraction concepts and skills learned in Module 3, opens the door to a wide variety of application word problems (5.NF.6).

Focus Standard:	5.NBT.7	Add, subtract, multiply, and divide decimals to hundredths, using concrete models or drawings and strategies based on place value, properties of operations, and/or the relationship between addition and subtraction; relate the strategy to a written method and explain the reasoning used.
	5.NF.4a	Apply and extend previous understandings of multiplication to multiply a fraction or whole number by a fraction.
		a. Interpret the product of *(a/b) × q* as *a* parts of a partition of *q* into *b* equal parts; equivalently, as the result of a sequence of operations *a × q ÷ b*. For example, use a visual fraction model to show (2/3) × 4 = 8/3, and create a story context for this equation. Do the same with (2/3) × (4/5) = 8/15. (In general, (a/b) × (c/d) = ac/bd.)
	5.NF.6	Solve real world problems involving multiplication of fractions and mixed numbers, e.g., by using visual fraction models or equations to represent the problem.
	5.MD.1	Convert among different-sized standard measurement units within a given measurement system (e.g., convert 5 cm to 0.05 m), and use these conversions in solving multistep, real world problems.
Instructional Days:	8	
Coherence		
Links from:	G4–M6	Decimal Fractions
	G5–M2	Multi-Digit Whole Number and Decimal Fraction Operations
Links to:	G6–M2	Arithmetic Operations Including Division by a Fraction
	G6–M4	Expressions and Equations

Objective 1: Multiply unit fractions by unit fractions.
(Lesson 13)

Objective 2: Multiply unit fractions by nonunit fractions.
(Lesson 14)

Objective 3: Multiply nonunit fractions by nonunit fractions.
(Lesson 15)

Objective 4: Solve word problems using tape diagrams and fraction-by-fraction multiplication.
(Lesson 16)

Objective 5: Relate decimal and fraction multiplication.
(Lessons 17 and 18)

Objective 6: Convert measures involving whole numbers, and solve multistep word problems.
(Lesson 19)

Objective 7: Convert mixed unit measurements, and solve multistep word problems.
(Lesson 20)

Topic F: Multiplication with Fractions and Decimals as Scaling and Word Problems

Students interpret multiplication in Grade 3 as equal groups, and in Grade 4 they begin to understand multiplication as comparison. Here, in Topic F, students once again extend their understanding of multiplication to include scaling (5.NF.5). Students compare the product to the size of one factor, given the size of the other factor (5.NF.5a) without calculation (e.g., 486 × 1,327.45 is twice as large as 243 × 1,327.45, because 486 = 2 × 243). This reasoning, along with the other work of this module, sets the stage for students to reason about the size of products when quantities are multiplied by 1, by numbers larger than 1, and by those smaller than 1. Students relate their previous work with equivalent fractions to interpreting multiplication by $\frac{n}{n}$ as multiplication by 1 (5.NF.5b).

Students build on their new understanding of fraction equivalence as multiplication by $\frac{n}{n}$ to convert fractions to decimals and decimals to fractions. For example, $\frac{3}{25}$ is easil renamed in hundredths as $\frac{12}{100}$ using multiplication of $\frac{4}{4}$. The word form of *twelve hundredths* will then be used to notate this quantity as a decimal. Conversions between fractional forms will be limited to fractions whose denominators are factors of 10, 100, or 1,000. Students will apply the concepts of the topic to real-world, multistep problems (5.NF.6).

Focus Standard:	5.NF.5	Interpret multiplication as scaling (resizing), by:
		a. Comparing the size of a product to the size of one factor on the basis of the size of the other factor, without performing the indicated multiplication.
		b. Explaining why multiplying a given number by a fraction greater than 1 results in a product greater than the given number (recognizing multiplication by whole numbers greater than 1 as a familiar case); explaining why multiplying a given number by a fraction less than 1 results in a product smaller than the given number; and relating the principle of fraction equivalence $a/b = (n × a)/(n × b)$ to the effect of multiplying a/b by 1.
	5.NF.6	Solve real world problems involving multiplication of fractions and mixed numbers, e.g., by using visual fraction models or equations to represent the problem.
Instructional Days:	4	
Coherence		
Links from:	G4–M3	Multi-Digit Multiplication and Division
	G5–M2	Multi-Digit Whole Number and Decimal Fraction Operations
Links to:	G6–M2	Arithmetic Operations Including Division by a Fraction
	G6–M4	Expressions and Equations

Objective 1: Explain the size of the product, and relate fraction and decimal equivalence to multiplying a fraction by 1.
(Lesson 21)

Objective 2: Compare the size of the product to the size of the factors.
(Lessons 22 and 23)

Objective 3: Solve word problems using fraction and decimal multiplication.
(Lesson 24)

Topic G: Division of Fractions and Decimal Fractions

Topic G begins the work of division with both fractions and decimal fractions. Students use tape diagrams and number lines to reason about the division of a whole number by a unit fraction and a unit fraction by a whole number (5.NF.7). Using the same thinking developed in Module 2 to divide whole numbers, they reason about how many fourths are in 5 when considering such cases as $5 \div \frac{1}{4}$. They also reason about the size of the unit when $\frac{1}{4}$ is partitioned into 5 equal parts: $\frac{1}{4} \div 5$. Using this thinking as a backdrop, students are introduced to decimal fraction divisors and use equivalent fraction and place value thinking to reason about the size of quotients, calculate quotients, and sensibly place the decimal in quotients (5.NBT.7).

Focus Standard:	5.OA.1	Use parentheses, brackets, or braces in numerical expressions, and evaluate expressions with these symbols.
	5.NBT.7	Add, subtract, multiply, and divide decimals to hundredths, using concrete models or drawings and strategies based on place value, properties of operations, and/or the relationship between addition and subtraction; relate the strategy to a written method and explain the reasoning used.
	5.NF.7	Apply and extend previous understandings of division to divide unit fractions by whole numbers and whole numbers by unit fractions. (Students able to multiple fractions in general can develop strategies to divide fractions in general, by reasoning about the relationship between multiplication and division. But division of a fraction by a fraction is not a requirement at this grade level.)
		a. Interpret division of a unit fraction by a non-zero whole number, and compute such quotients. *For example, create a story context for (1/3) ÷ 4, and use a visual fraction model to show the quotient. Use the relationship between multiplication and division to explain that (1/3) ÷ 4 = 1/12 because (1/12) × 4 = 1/3.*
		b. Interpret division of a whole number by a unit fraction, and compute such quotients. *For example, create a story context for 4 ÷ (1/5), and use a visual fraction model to show the quotient. Use the relationship between multiplication and division to explain that 4 ÷ (1/5) = 20 because 20 × (1/5) = 4.*
		c. Solve real world problems involving division of unit fractions by non-zero whole numbers and division of whole numbers by unit fractions, e.g., by using visual fraction models and equations to represent the problem. *For example, how much chocolate will each person get if 3 people share 1/2 lb of chocolate equally? How many 1/3-cup servings are in 2 cups of raisins?*
Instructional Days:	7	
Coherence		
Links from:	G4–M5	Fraction Equivalence, Ordering, and Operations
	G5–M2	Multi-Digit Whole Number and Decimal Fraction Operations
Links to:	G6–M2	Arithmetic Operations Including Division by a Fraction
	G6–M4	Expressions and Equations

Objective 1: Divide a whole number by a unit fraction.
(Lesson 25)

Objective 2: Divide a unit fraction by a whole number.
(Lesson 26)

Objective 3: Solve problems involving fraction division.
(Lesson 27)

Objective 4: Write equations and word problems corresponding to tape and number line diagrams.
(Lesson 28)

Objective 5: Connect division by a unit fraction to division by 1 tenth and 1 hundredth.
(Lesson 29)

Objective 6: Divide decimal dividends by nonunit decimal divisors.
(Lessons 30 and 31)

Topic H: Interpretation of Numerical Expressions

The module concludes with Topic H, in which numerical expressions involving fraction-by-fraction multiplication are interpreted and evaluated (5.OA.1, 5.OA.2). Students create and solve word problems involving both multiplication and division of fractions and decimal fractions.

Focus Standard:	5.OA.1	Use parentheses, brackets, or braces in numerical expressions, and evaluate expressions with these symbols.
	5.OA.2	Write simple expressions that record calculations with numbers, and interpret numerical expressions without evaluating them. *For example, express the calculation "add 8 and 7, then multiply by 2" as 2 × (8 +7). Recognize that 3 × (18,932 + 921) is three times as large as 18,932 + 921, without having to calculate the indicated sum or product.*
Instructional Days:	2	
Coherence		
Links from:	G4–M5	Fraction Equivalence, Ordering, and Operations
	G5–M2	Multi-Digit Whole Number and Decimal Fraction Operations
Links to:	G6–M2	Arithmetic Operations Including Division by a Fraction
	G6–M4	Expressions and Operations.

Objective 1: Interpret and evaluate numerical expressions including the language of scaling and fraction division.
(Lesson 32)

Objective 2: Create story contexts for numerical expressions and tape diagrams, and solve word problems.
(Lesson 33)

MODULE 5: ADDITION AND MULTIPLICATION WITH VOLUME AND AREA

OVERVIEW

In this 25-day module, students work with two- and three-dimensional figures. Volume is introduced to students through concrete exploration of cubic units and culminates with the development of the volume formula for right rectangular prisms. The second half of the module turns to extending students' understanding of two-dimensional figures. Students combine prior knowledge of area with newly acquired knowledge of fraction multiplication to determine the area of rectangular figures with fractional side lengths. They then engage in hands-on construction of two-dimensional shapes, developing a foundation for classifying the shapes by reasoning about their attributes. This module fills a gap between Grade 4's work with two-dimensional figures and Grade 6's work with volume and area.

In Topic A, students extend their spatial structuring to three dimensions through an exploration of volume. They come to see volume as an attribute of solid figures and understand that cubic units are used to measure it (5.MD.3). Using improvised, customary, and metric units, they build three-dimensional shapes, including right rectangular prisms, and count units to find the volume (5.MD.4). By developing a systematic approach to counting the unit cubes, students make connections between area and volume. They partition a rectangular prism into layers of unit cubes and reason that the number of unit cubes in a single layer corresponds to the number of unit squares on a face. They begin to conceptualize the layers themselves, oriented in any one of three directions, as iterated units. This understanding allows students to reason about containers formed by nets, reasonably predict the number of cubes required to fill them, and test their prediction by packing the container.

Concrete understanding of volume and multiplicative reasoning (5.MD.3) comes together in Topic B as the systematic counting from Topic A leads naturally to formulas for finding the volume of a right rectangular prism (5.MD.5). Students solidify the connection between volume as *packing* and volume as *filling* by comparing the amount of liquid that fills a container to the number of cubes that can be packed into it. This connection is formalized as students see that 1 cubic centimeter is equal to 1 milliliter. Complexity increases as students use their knowledge that volume is additive to partition and calculate the total volume of solid figures composed of nonoverlapping, rectangular prisms. Word problems involving the volume of rectangular prisms with whole number edge lengths solidify understanding and give students opportunity to reason about scaling in the context of volume. This topic concludes with a design project that gives students the opportunity to apply the concepts and formulas they have learned throughout Topics A and B to create a sculpture of a specified volume composed of varied rectangular prisms with parameters given in the project description.

In Topic C, students extend their understanding of area as they use rulers and set squares to construct and measure rectangles with fractional side lengths and find their areas. They apply their extensive knowledge of fraction multiplication to interpret areas of rectangles with fractional side lengths (5.NF.4b) and solve real-world problems involving these figures (5.NF.6), including reasoning about scaling through contexts in which volumes are compared. Visual models and equations are used to represent the problems through the read-draw-write protocol.

In Topic D, students draw two-dimensional shapes in order to analyze their attributes and use those attributes to classify them. Familiar figures, such as parallelograms, rhombuses, squares, and trapezoids, have all been defined in earlier grades, and by Grade 4, students have gained an understanding of shapes beyond the intuitive level. Grade 5 extends this understanding through an in-depth analysis of the properties and defining attributes of quadrilaterals. Grade 4's work with the protractor is applied in order to construct various quadrilaterals. Using measurement tools illuminates the attributes used to define and recognize each quadrilateral (5.G.3). Students see, for example, that the same process that they used to construct a parallelogram will also produce a rectangle when all angles are constructed to measure 90 degrees. Students then analyze defining attributes and create a hierarchical classification of quadrilaterals (5.G.4).

FOCUS GRADE-LEVEL STANDARDS

Apply and extend previous understandings of multiplication and division to multiply and divide fractions.[6]

5.NF.4 Apply and extend previous understandings of multiplication to multiply a fraction or whole number by a fraction.

b. Find the area of a rectangle with fractional side lengths by tiling it with unit squares of the appropriate unit fraction side lengths, and show that the area is the same as would be found by multiplying the side lengths. Multiply fractional side lengths to find areas of rectangles, and represent fraction products as rectangular areas.

5.NF.6 Solve real world problems involving multiplication of fractions and mixed numbers, e.g., by using visual fraction models or equations to represent the problem.

Geometric measurement: understand concepts of volume and relate volume to multiplication and addition.

5.MD.3 Recognize volume as an attribute of solid figures and understand concepts of volume measurement.

    a.   A cube with side length 1 unit, called a "unit cube," is said to have "one cubic unit" of volume, and can be used to measure volume.

    b.   A solid figure which can be packed without gaps or overlaps using n unit cubes is said to have a volume of n cubic units.

5.MD.4 Measure volumes by counting unit cubes, using cubic cm, cubic in, cubic ft, and improvised units.

5.MD.5 Relate volume to the operations of multiplication and addition and solve real world and mathematical problems involving volume.

    a.   Find the volume of a right rectangular prism with whole-number side lengths by packing it with unit cubes, and show that the volume is the same as would be found by multiplying the edge lengths, equivalently by multiplying the height by the area of the base. Represent threefold whole-number products as volumes, e.g., to represent the associative property of multiplication.

    b.   Apply the formulas $V = l \times w \times h$ and $V = b \times h$ for rectangular prisms to find volumes of right rectangular prisms with whole-number edge lengths in the context of solving real world and mathematical problems.

    c.   Recognize volume as additive. Find volumes of solid figures composed of two non-overlapping right rectangular prisms by adding the volumes of the non-overlapping parts, applying this technique to solve real world problems.

Classify two-dimensional figures into categories based on their properties.

5.G.3 Understand that attributes belonging to a category of two-dimensional figures also belong to all subcategories of that category. *For example, all rectangles have four right angles and squares are rectangles, so all squares have four right angles.*

5.G.4 Classify two-dimensional figures in a hierarchy based on properties.

FOUNDATIONAL STANDARDS

3.MD.5 Recognize area as an attribute of plane figures and understand concepts of area measurement.

    a.   A square with side length 1 unit, called "a unit square," is said to have "one square unit" of area, and can be used to measure area.

    b.   A plane figure which can be covered without gaps or overlaps by n unit squares is said to have an area of n square units.

4.MD.3 Apply the area and perimeter formulas for rectangles in real world and mathematical problems. For example, find the width of a rectangular room given the area of the flooring and the length, by viewing the area formula as a multiplication equation with an unknown factor.

4.MD.5 Recognize angles as geometric shapes that are formed wherever two rays share a common endpoint, and understand concepts of angle measurement:

  a.   An angle is measured with reference to a circle with its center at the common endpoint of the rays, by considering the fraction of the circular arc between the points where the two rays intersect the circle. An angle that turns through 1/360 of a circle is called a "one-degree angle," and can be used to measure angles.

  b.   An angle that turns through n one-degree angles is said to have an angle measure of n degrees.

4.MD.6 Measure angles in whole-number degrees using a protractor. Sketch angles of specified measure.

4.MD.7 Recognize angle measure as additive. When an angle is decomposed into non-overlapping parts, the angle measure of the whole is the sum of the angle measures of the parts. Solve addition and subtraction problems to find unknown angles on a diagram in real world and mathematical problems, e.g., by using an equation with a symbol for the unknown angle measure.

3.G.1 Understand that shapes in different categories (e.g., rhombuses, rectangles, and others) may share attributes (e.g., having four sides), and that the shared attributes can define a larger category (e.g., quadrilaterals). Recognize rhombuses, rectangles, and squares as examples of quadrilaterals, and draw examples of quadrilaterals that do not belong to any of these subcategories.

4.G.1 Draw points, lines, line segments, rays, angles (right, acute, obtuse), and perpendicular and parallel lines. Identify these in two-dimensional figures.

4.G.2 Classify two-dimensional figures based on the presence or absence of parallel or perpendicular lines, or the presence or absence of angles of a specified size. Recognize right triangles as a category, and identify right triangles.

5.NF.4 Apply and extend previous understandings of multiplication to multiply a fraction or whole number by a fraction.

  a.   Interpret the product $(a/b) \times q$ as a parts of a partition of q into b equal parts; equivalently, as the result of a sequence of operations $a \times q \div b$. *For example, use a visual fraction model to show* $(2/3) \times 4 = 8/3$, *and create a story context for this equation. Do the same with* $(2/3) \times (4/5) = 8/15$. *(In general,* $(a/b) \times (c/d) = ac/bd$.*)*

FOCUS STANDARDS FOR MATHEMATICAL PRACTICE

MP.1 *Make sense of problems and persevere in solving them.* Students work toward a solid understanding of volume through the design and construction of a three-dimensional sculpture within given parameters.

MP.2 *Reason abstractly and quantitatively.* Students make sense of quantities and their relationships when they analyze a geometric shape or real-life scenario and identify, represent, and manipulate the relevant measurements. Students decontextualize when they represent geometric figures symbolically and apply formulas.

MP.3 *Construct viable arguments and critique the reasoning of others.* Students analyze shapes, draw conclusions, and recognize and use counterexamples as they classify two-dimensional figures in a hierarchy based on properties.

MP.4 *Model with mathematics.* Students model with mathematics as they make connections between addition and multiplication as applied to volume and area. They represent the area and volume of geometric figures with equations, and vice versa, and represent fraction products with rectangular areas. Students apply concepts of volume and area and their knowledge of fractions to design a sculpture based on given mathematical parameters. Through their work analyzing and classifying two-dimensional shapes, students draw conclusions about their relationships and continuously see how mathematical concepts can be modeled geometrically.

MP.6 *Attend to precision.* Mathematically proficient students try to communicate precisely with others. They endeavor to use clear definitions in discussion with others and in their own reasoning. Students state the meaning of the symbols they choose, including using the equal sign consistently and appropriately. They are careful about specifying units of measure and labeling axes to clarify the correspondence with quantities in a problem. They calculate accurately and efficiently, expressing numerical answers with a degree of precision appropriate for the problem context. In the elementary grades, students give carefully formulated explanations to each other. By the time they reach high school, they have learned to examine claims and make explicit use of definitions.

MP.7 *Look for and make use of structure.* Students discern patterns and structures as they apply additive and multiplicative reasoning to determine volumes. They relate multiplying two of the dimensions of a rectangular prism to determining how many cubic units would be in each layer of the prism and relate the third dimension to determining how many layers there are in the prism. This understanding supports students in seeing why volume can be computed as the product of three length measurements or as the product of one area by one length measurement. In addition, recognizing that volume is additive allows students to find the total volume of solid figures composed of more than one nonoverlapping right rectangular prism.

MODULE TOPIC SUMMARIES

Topic A: Concepts of Volume

In Topic A, students extend their spatial structuring to three dimensions through an exploration of volume. They come to see volume as an attribute of solid figures and understand that cubic units are used to measure it (5.MD.3). Using unit cubes, both customary and metric, students build three-dimensional shapes, including right rectangular prisms, and count to find the volume (5.MD.4). By developing a systematic approach to counting the unit cubes, they make connections between area and volume.

Next, students pack rectangular prisms made from nets with centimeter cubes. This helps them to visualize the layers of cubic units that compose volumes, an understanding that allows them to reasonably predict the number of cubes required to fill the containers and then test their predictions by packing the containers. Finally, students compose and decompose a rectangular prism from and into layers of unit cubes, and reason that the number of unit cubes in a single layer corresponds to the number of unit squares on a face. They begin to conceptualize the layers themselves, oriented in any one of three directions, as iterated units.

Focus Standard:	5.MD.3	Recognize volume as an attribute of solid figures and understand concepts of volume measurement.
		a. A cube with side length 1 unit, called a "unit cube," is said to have "one cubic unit" of volume, and can be used to measure volume.
		b. A solid figure which can be packed without gaps or overlaps using n unit cubes is said to have a volume of n cubic units.
	5.MD.4	Measure volumes by counting unit cubes, using cubic cm, cubic in, cubic ft, and improvised units.
Instructional Days:	3	
Coherence		
Links from:	G2–M8	Time, Shapes, and Fractions as Equal Parts of Shapes
	G3–M4	Multiplication and Area
	G3–M5	Fractions as Numbers on the Number Line
Links to:	G6–M5	Area, Surface Area, and Volume Problems

Objective 1: Explore volume by building with and counting unit cubes.
(Lesson 1)

Objective 2: Find the volume of a right rectangular prism by packing with cubic units and counting.
(Lesson 2)

Objective 3: Compose and decompose right rectangular prisms using layers.
(Lesson 3)

Topic B: Volume and the Operations of Multiplication and Addition

Concrete understanding of volume and multiplicative reasoning (5.MD.3) come together in Topic B as the systematic counting from Topic A leads naturally to formulas for finding the volume of a right rectangular prism (5.MD.5). Students come to see that multiplying the edge lengths or multiplying the height by the area of the base yields an equivalent volume to that found by packing and counting unit cubes.

Next, students solidify the connection between volume as *packing* with volume as *filling* by comparing the amount of liquid that fills a container to the number of cubes that can be packed into it. This connection is formalized as students see that 1 cubic centimeter is equal to 1 milliliter. Complexity increases as students use their knowledge that volume is additive to partition and calculate the total volume of solid figures composed of nonoverlapping rectangular prisms.

Word problems involving the volume of rectangular prisms with whole number edge lengths solidify understanding and give students opportunity to reason about scaling in the context of volume. This topic concludes with a design project that allows students to apply the concepts and formulas they have learned throughout Topics A and B to create a sculpture of a specified volume composed of varied rectangular prisms with parameters stipulated in the project description.

Focus Standard:	5.MD.3	Recognize volume as an attribute of solid figures and understand concepts of volume measurement.
		c. A cube with side length 1 unit, called a "unit cube," is said to have "one cubic unit" of volume, and can be used to measure volume.
		d. A solid figure which can be packed without gaps or overlaps using *n* unit cubes is said to have a volume of *n* cubic units.
	5.MD.5	Relate volume to the operations of multiplication and addition and solve real world and mathematical problems involving volume.
		a. Find the volume of a right rectangular prism with whole-number side lengths by packing it with unit cubes, and show that the volume is the same as would be found by multiplying the edge lengths, equivalently by multiplying the height by the area of the base. Represent threefold whole-number products as volume, e.g., to represent the associative property of multiplication.
		b. Apply the formulas $V = l \times w \times h$ and $V = b \times h$ for rectangular prisms to find volumes of right rectangular prisms with whole-number edge lengths in the context of solving real world and mathematical problems.
		c. Recognize volume as additive. Find volumes of solid figures composed of two non-overlapping right rectangular prisms by adding the volumes of the non-overlapping parts, applying this technique to solve real world problems.
Instructional Days:	6	
Coherence		
Links from:	G3–M4	Multiplication and Area
Links to:	G6–M5	Area, Surface Area, and Volume Problems

Objective 1: Use multiplication to calculate volume.
(Lesson 4)

Objective 2: Use multiplication to connect volume as *packing* with volume as *filling*.
(Lesson 5)

Objective 2: Find the total volume of solid figures composed of two nonoverlapping rectangular prisms.
(Lesson 6)

Objective 3: Solve word problems involving the volume of rectangular prisms with whole number edge lengths.
(Lesson 7)

Objective 4: Apply concepts and formulas of volume to design a sculpture using rectangular prisms within given parameters.
(Lessons 8 and 9)

Topic C: Area of Rectangular Figures with Fractional Side Lengths

In Topic C, students extend their understanding of area as they use rulers and right angle templates to construct and measure rectangles with fractional side lengths and find their areas. They apply their extensive knowledge of fraction multiplication to interpret areas of rectangles with fractional side lengths (5.NF.4b) and solve real-world problems involving these figures (5.NF.6), including reasoning about scaling through contexts in which areas are compared. Visual models and equations are used to represent the problems through the Read-Draw-Write protocol.

Focus Standard:	5.NF.4b	Apply and extend previous understanding of multiplication to multiply a fraction or whole number by a fraction.
		b. Find the area of a rectangle with fractional side lengths by tiling it with unit squares of the appropriate unit fraction side lengths, and show that the area is the same as would be found by multiplying the side lengths. Multiply fractional side lengths to find areas of rectangles, and represent fraction products as rectangular areas.
	5.NF.6	Solve real world problems involving multiplication of fractions and mixed numbers, e.g., by using visual fraction models or equations to represent the problem.
Instructional Days:	6	
Coherence		
Links from:	G4–M4	Angle Measure and Plane Figures
Links to:	G6–M2	Arithmetic Operations Including Division of Fractions

Objective 1: Find the area of rectangles with whole-by-mixed and whole-by-fractional number side lengths by tiling, record by drawing, and relate to fraction multiplication.
(Lesson 10)

Objective 2: Find the area of rectangles with mixed-by-mixed and fractional-by-fractional side lengths by tiling, record by drawing, and relate to fraction multiplication.
(Lesson 11)

Objective 3: Measure to find the area of rectangles with fractional side lengths.
(Lesson 12)

Objective 4: Multiply mixed-number factors, and relate to the distributive property and the area model.
(Lesson 13)

Objective 5: Solve real-world problems involving area of figures with fractional side lengths using visual models or equations, or both.
(Lessons 14 and 15)

Topic D: Drawing, Analysis, and Classification of Two-Dimensional Shapes

In Topic D, students draw two-dimensional shapes in order to analyze their attributes and then use those attributes to classify them. Familiar figures such as parallelograms, rhombuses, squares, and trapezoids have all been defined in earlier grades, and by Grade 4, students have gained an understanding of shapes beyond the intuitive level. Grade 5 extends this understanding through an in-depth analysis of the properties and defining attributes of quadrilaterals.

The work in Grade 4 with the protractor is applied in this topic in order to construct various quadrilaterals. Using measurement tools illuminates the attributes used to define and recognize each quadrilateral (5.G.3). Students see, for example, that the same process that they used to construct a parallelogram will also produce a rectangle when all angles are constructed to measure 90 degrees. Students then analyze defining attributes and create a hierarchical classification of quadrilaterals (5.G.4).

Focus Standard:	5.G.3	Understand that attributes belonging to a category of two-dimensional figures also belong to all subcategories of that category. *For example, all rectangles have four right angles and squares are rectangles, so all squares have four right angles.*
	5.G.4	Classify two-dimensional figures in a hierarchy based on properties.
Instructional Days:	6	
Coherence		
Links from:	G3–M7	Geometry and Measurement Word Problems
	G4–M4	Angle Measure and Plane Figures
Links to:	G6–M4	Expressions and Equations

Objective 1: Draw trapezoids to clarify their attributes, and define trapezoids based on those attributes.
(Lesson 16)

Objective 2: Draw parallelograms to clarify their attributes, and define parallelograms based on those attributes.
(Lesson 17)

Objective 3: Draw rectangles and rhombuses to clarify their attributes, and define rectangles and rhombuses based on those attributes.
(Lesson 18)

Objective 4: Draw kites and squares to clarify their attributes, and define kites and squares based on those attributes.
(Lesson 19)

Objective 5: Classify two-dimensional figures in a hierarchy based on properties.
(Lesson 20)

Objective 6: Draw and identify varied two-dimensional figures from given attributes.
(Lesson 21)

MODULE 6: PROBLEM SOLVING WITH THE COORDINATE PLANE

OVERVIEW

In this 40-day module, students develop a coordinate system for the first quadrant of the coordinate plane and use it to solve problems. Students use the familiar number line as an introduction to the idea of a coordinate and construct two perpendicular number lines to create a coordinate system on the plane. They see that just as points on the line can be located by their distance from zero, the plane's coordinate system can be used to locate and plot points using two coordinates. They then use the coordinate system to explore relationships between points, ordered pairs, patterns, lines and, more abstractly, the rules that generate them. This study culminates in an exploration of the coordinate plane in real-world applications.

In Topic A, students come to realize that any line, regardless of orientation, can be made into a number line by first locating zero, choosing a unit length, and partitioning the length unit into fractional lengths as desired. They are introduced to the concept of a coordinate as describing the distance of a point on the line from zero. As students construct these number lines in various orientations on a plane, they explore ways to describe the position of points *not* located on the lines. This discussion leads to the discovery that a second number line, perpendicular to the first, creates an efficient, precise way to describe the location of these points. Thus, points can be located using coordinate pairs, (a, b) by starting at the origin, traveling a distance of a units along the x-axis and b units along a line parallel to the y-axis. Students describe given points using coordinate pairs as well as use given coordinate pairs to plot points (5.G.1). The topic concludes with an investigation of patterns in coordinate pairs along lines parallel to the axes, which leads to the discovery that these lines consist of the set of points whose distance from the x- or y-axis is constant.

Students move on to plotting points and using them to draw lines in the plane in Topic B (5.G.1). They investigate patterns relating the x - and y-coordinates of the points on the line and reason about the patterns in the ordered pairs, laying important groundwork for Grade 6 proportional reasoning. Topic B continues as students use given rules (e.g., multiply by 2, and then add 3) to generate coordinate pairs, plot points, and investigate relationships. Patterns in the resultant coordinate pairs are analyzed, leading students to discover that such rules produce collinear sets of points. Students next generate two number patterns from two given rules, plot the points, and analyze the relationships within the sequences of the ordered pairs (5.OA.3). Patterns continue to be the focus as students analyze the effect on the steepness of the line when the second coordinate is produced through an addition rule as opposed to a multiplication rule (5.OA.2, 5.OA.3). Students also create rules to generate number patterns, plot the points, connect those points with lines, and look for intersections.

Topic C finds students drawing figures in the coordinate plane by plotting points to create parallel, perpendicular, and intersecting lines. They reason about what points are needed to produce such lines and angles, and then investigate the resultant points and their relationships. Students also reason about the relationships among coordinate pairs that are symmetric about a line (5.G.1).

Problem solving in the coordinate plane is the focus of Topic D. Students draw symmetric figures using both angle size and distance from a given line of symmetry (5.G.2). Line graphs are also used to explore patterns and make predictions based on those patterns (5.G.2, 5.OA.3). To round out the topic, students use coordinate planes to solve real-world problems.

Topic E provides an opportunity for students to encounter complex, multistep problems requiring the application of concepts and skills they mastered throughout the Grade 5 curriculum. They use all four operations with both whole numbers and fractions in varied contexts. The problems in Topic E are designed to be nonroutine, requiring students to persevere in order to solve them. While wrestling with complexity is an important part of Topic E, the true strength of this topic is derived from the time allocated for students to construct arguments and critique the reasoning of their classmates. After students have been given adequate time to ponder and solve the problems, two lessons are devoted to sharing approaches and solutions. Students will partner to justify their conclusions, communicate them to others, and respond to the arguments of their peers.

In this final topic of Module 6, and in fact, A *Story of Units*, students spend time producing a compendium of their learning. They not only reach back to recall learning from the very beginning of Grade 5, but they also expand their thinking by exploring such concepts as the Fibonacci sequence. Students solidify the year's learning by creating and playing games, exploring patterns as they reflect back on their elementary years. All materials for the games and activities are then housed for summer use in boxes that the students create in the final two lessons of the year.

FOCUS GRADE-LEVEL STANDARDS

Write and interpret numerical expressions.

5.OA.2 Write simple expressions that record calculations with numbers, and interpret numerical expressions without evaluating them. *For example, express the calculation "add 8 and 7, then multiply by 2" as $2 \times (8 + 7)$. Recognize that $3 \times (18,932 + 921)$ is three times as large as 18,932 + 921, without having to calculate the indicated sum or product.*

Analyze patterns and relationships.

5.OA.3 Generate two numerical patterns using two given rules. Identify apparent relationships between corresponding terms. Form ordered pairs consisting of corresponding terms from the two patterns, and graph the ordered pairs on a coordinate plane. *For example, given the rule "Add 3" and the starting number 0, and given the rule "Add 6" and the starting number 0, generate terms in the resulting sequences, and observe that the terms in one sequence are twice the corresponding terms in the other sequence. Explain informally why this is so.*

Graph points on the coordinate plane to solve real world and mathematical problems.

5.G.1 Use a pair of perpendicular number lines, called axes, to define a coordinate system, with the intersection of the lines (the origin) arranged to coincide with the 0 on each line and a given point in the plane located by using an ordered pair of numbers, called its coordinates. Understand that the first number indicates how far to travel from the origin in the direction of one axis, and the second number indicates how far to travel in the direction of the second axis, with the convention that the names of the two axes and the coordinates correspond (e.g., x-axis and x-coordinate, y-axis and y-coordinate).

5.G.2 Represent real world and mathematical problems by graphing points in the first quadrant of the coordinate plane, and interpret coordinate values of points in the context of the situation.

FOUNDATIONAL STANDARDS

4.OA.1 Interpret a multiplication equation as a comparison, e.g., interpret $35 = 5 \times 7$ as a statement that 35 is 5 times as many as 7 and 7 times as many as 5. Represent verbal statements of multiplicative comparisons as multiplication equations.

4.OA.5 Generate a number or shape pattern that follows a given rule. Identify apparent features of the pattern that were not explicit in the rule itself. *For example, given the rule "Add 3" and the starting number 1, generate terms in the resulting sequence and observe that the terms appear to alternate between odd and even numbers. Explain informally why the numbers will continue to alternate in this way.*

4.MD.5 Recognize angles as geometric shapes that are formed wherever two rays share a common endpoint, and understand concepts of angle measurement:

a. An angle is measured with reference to a circle with its center at the common endpoint of the rays, by considering the fraction of the circular arc between the points where the two rays intersect the circle. An angle that turns through 1/360 of a circle is called a "one-degree angle," and can be used to measure angles.

b. An angle that turns through n one-degree angles is said to have an angle measure of n degrees.

4.MD.6 Measure angles in whole-number degrees using a protractor. Sketch angles of specified measure.

4.MD.7 Recognize angle measure as additive. When an angle is decomposed into non-overlapping parts, the angle measure of the whole is the sum of the angle measures of the parts. Solve addition and subtraction problems to find unknown angles on a diagram in real world and mathematical problems, e.g., by using an equation with a symbol for the unknown angle measure.

4.G.1 Draw points, lines, line segments, rays, angles (right, acute, obtuse), and perpendicular and parallel lines. Identify these in two-dimensional figures.

5.NF.2 Solve word problems involving addition and subtraction of fractions referring to the same whole, including cases of unlike denominators, e.g., by using visual fraction models or equations to represent the problem. Use benchmark fractions and number sense of fractions to estimate mentally and assess the reasonableness of answers. *For example, recognize an incorrect result 2/5 + 1/2 = 3/7, by observing that 3/7 < 1/2.*

5.NF.3 Interpret a fraction as division of the numerator by the denominator ($a/b = a \div b$). Solve word problems involving division of whole numbers leading to answers in the form of fractions or mixed numbers, e.g., by using visual fraction models or equations to represent the problem. *For example, interpret 3/4 as the result of dividing 3 by 4, noting that 3/4 multiplied by 4 equals 3, and that when 3 wholes are shared equally among 4 people each person has a share of size 3/4. If 9 people want to share a 50-pound sack of rice equally by weight, how many pounds of rice should each person get? Between what two whole numbers does your answer lie?*

5.NF.6 Solve real world problems involving multiplication of fractions and mixed numbers, e.g., by using visual fraction models or equations to represent the problem.

5.NF.7c Apply and extend previous understandings of division to divide unit fractions by whole numbers and whole numbers by unit fractions.

  c. Solve real world problems involving division of a unit fractions by non-zero whole numbers and division of whole numbers by unit fractions, e.g., by using visual fraction models and equations to represent the problem. *For example, how much chocolate will each person get if 3 people share 1/2 lb of chocolate equally? How many 1/3-cup servings are in 2 cups of raisins?*

5.MD.1 Convert among different-sized standard measurement units within a given measurement system (e.g., convert 5 cm to 0.05 m), and use these conversions in solving multistep, real world problems.

5.MD.5 Relate volume to the operations of multiplication and addition and solve real world and mathematical problems involving volume.

FOCUS STANDARDS FOR MATHEMATICAL PRACTICE

MP.1 *Make sense of problems and persevere in solving them.* Students make sense of problems as they use tape diagrams and other models, persevering to solve complex, multistep word problems. Students check their work and monitor their own progress, assessing their approach and its validity within the given context and altering their method when necessary.

MP.2 *Reason abstractly and quantitatively.* Students reason abstractly and quantitatively as they interpret the steepness and orientation of a line given by the points of a number pattern. Students attend to the meaning of the values in an ordered pair and reason about how they can be manipulated in order to create parallel, perpendicular, or intersecting lines.

MP.3 *Construct viable arguments and critique the reasoning of others.* As students construct a coordinate system on a plane, they generate explanations about the best place to create a second line of coordinates. They analyze lines and the coordinate pairs that comprise them and then draw conclusions and construct arguments about their positioning on the coordinate plane. Students also critique the reasoning of others and construct viable arguments as they analyze classmates' solutions to lengthy, multistep word problems.

MP.6 *Attend to precision.* Mathematically proficient students try to communicate precisely to others. They endeavor to use clear definitions in discussion with others and in their own reasoning. These students state the meaning of the symbols they choose, including using the equal sign, consistently and appropriately. They are careful about specifying units of measure and labeling axes to clarify the correspondence with quantities in a problem. The students calculate accurately and efficiently, expressing numerical answers with a degree of precision appropriate for the problem context. In the elementary grades, students give carefully formulated explanations to each other. By the time they reach high school, they have learned to examine claims and make explicit use of definitions.

MP.7 *Look for and make use of structure.* Students identify and create patterns in coordinate pairs and make predictions about their effect on the lines that connect them. Students also recognize patterns in sets of coordinate pairs and use those patterns to explain why a line is parallel or perpendicular to an axis. They use operational rules to generate coordinate pairs and, conversely, generalize observed patterns within coordinate pairs as rules.

MODULE TOPIC SUMMARIES

Topic A: Coordinate Systems

In Topic A, students revisit a Grade 3 activity in which they use lined paper to subdivide a length into n equal parts. In Grade 5, this activity is extended as students explore that any line, regardless of orientation, can be made into a number line by first locating zero, choosing a unit length, and partitioning the length unit into fractional lengths. Students are introduced to the concept of a coordinate as describing the distance of a point on the line from zero.

As they construct these number lines in various orientations on a plane, students explore ways to describe the position of points not located on the lines. This discussion leads to the discovery that a second number line, perpendicular to the first, creates an efficient, precise way to describe the location of these points. Thus, points can be located using coordinate pairs (a, b), by traveling a distance of a units from the origin along the x-axis and b units along a line parallel to the y-axis.

Students describe given points using coordinate pairs and then use given coordinate pairs to plot points (5.G.1). The topic concludes with an investigation of the patterns in coordinate pairs along vertical or horizontal lines, which leads to the discovery that these lines consist of the set of points whose distance from the x- or y-axis is constant.

Focus Standard:	5.G.1	Use a pair of perpendicular number lines, called axes, to define a coordinate system, with the intersection of the lines (the origin) arranged to coincide with the 0 on each line and a given point in the plane located by using an ordered pair of numbers, called its coordinates. Understand that the first number indicates how far to travel from the origin in the direction of one axis, and the second number indicates how far to travel in the direction of the second axis, with the convention that the names of the two axes and the coordinates correspond (e.g., x-axis and x-coordinate, y-axis and y-coordinate).
Instructional Days:	6	
Coherence		
Links from:	G3–M5	Fractions as Numbers on the Number Line
Links to:	G6–M1	Ratios and Unit Rates
	G6–M3	Rational Numbers

Objective 1: Construct a coordinate system on a line.
(Lesson 1)

Objective 2: Construct a coordinate system on a plane.
(Lesson 2)

Objective 3: Name points using coordinate pairs, and use the coordinate pairs to plot points.
(Lessons 3 and 4)

Objective 4: Investigate patterns in vertical and horizontal lines, and interpret points on the plane as distances from the axes.
(Lessons 5 and 6)

Topic B: Patterns in the Coordinate Plane and Graphing Number Patterns from Rules

In Topic B, students plot points and use them to draw lines in the plane (5.G.1). Students begin by investigating patterns relating the x- and y-coordinates of the points on the line and reasoning about the patterns in the ordered pairs, which lays important groundwork for Grade 6 work with proportional reasoning. Topic B continues as students use given rules (e.g., multiply by 2, and then add 3) to generate coordinate pairs, plot points, and investigate relationships. Patterns in the resultant coordinate pairs are analyzed to discover that such rules produce collinear sets of points, or lines. Students next generate two number patterns from two given rules, plot the points, and analyze the relationships within the sequences of the ordered pairs and the graphs (5.OA.3). Patterns continue to be the focus as students analyze the effect on the steepness of the line when the second coordinate is produced through an addition rule as opposed to a multiplication rule (5.OA.3). They also create rules to generate number patterns, plot the points, connect those points with lines, and look for intersections.

Focus Standard:	5.OA.2	Write simple expressions that record calculations with numbers, and interpret numerical expressions without evaluating them. *For example, express the calculation "add 8 and 7, then multiply by 2" as 2 × (8 + 7). Recognize that 3 × (18,932 + 921) is three times as large as 18,932 + 921, without having to calculate the indicated sum or product.*
	5.OA.3	Generate two numerical patterns using two given rules. Identify apparent relationships between corresponding terms. Form ordered pairs consisting of corresponding terms from the two patterns, and graph the ordered pairs on a coordinate plane. *For example, given the rule "Add 3" and the starting number 0, and given the rule "Add 6" and the starting number 0, generate terms in the resulting sequences, and observe that the terms in one sequence are twice the corresponding terms in the other sequence. Explain informally why this is so.*
	5.G.1	Use a pair of perpendicular number lines, called axes, to define a coordinate system, with the intersection of the lines (the origin) arranged to coincide with the 0 on each line and a given point in the plane located by using an ordered pair of numbers, called its coordinates. Understand that the first number indicates how far to travel from the origin in the direction of one axis, and the second number indicates how far to travel in the direction of the second axis, with the convention that the names of the two axes and the coordinates correspond (e.g., x-axis and x-coordinate, y-axis and y-coordinate).
Instructional Days:	6	
Coherence		
Links from:	G4–M4	Angle Measure and Plane Figures
	G4–M7	Exploring Measurement with Multiplication
Links to:	G6–M1	Ratios and Unit Rates
	G6–M3	Rational Numbers
	G6–M4	Expressions and Equations

Objective 1: Plot points, use them to draw lines in the plane, and describe patterns within the coordinate pairs.
(Lesson 7)

Objective 2: Generate a number pattern from a given rule, and plot the points.
(Lesson 8)

Objective 3: Generate two number patterns from given rules, plot the points, and analyze the patterns.
(Lesson 9)

Objective 4: Compare the lines and patterns generated by addition rules and multiplication rules.
(Lesson 10)

Objective 5: Analyze number patterns created from mixed operations.
(Lesson 11)

Objective 6: Create a rule to generate a number pattern, and plot the points.
(Lesson 12)

Topic C: Drawing Figures in the Coordinate Plane

In Topic C, students draw figures in the coordinate plane by plotting points to create parallel, perpendicular, and intersecting lines. They reason about what points are needed to produce such lines and angles, and investigate the resultant points and their relationships. In preparation for Topic D, students recall Grade 4 concepts such as angles on a line, angles at a point, and vertical angles—all produced by plotting points and drawing figures on the coordinate plane (5.G.1). To conclude the topic, students draw symmetric figures using both angle size and distance from a given line of symmetry (5.G.2).

Focus Standard:	5.G.1	Use a pair of perpendicular number lines, called axes, to define a coordinate system, with the intersection of the lines (the origin) arranged to coincide with the 0 on each line and a given point in the plane located by using an ordered pair of numbers, called its coordinates. Understand that the first number indicates how far to travel from the origin in the direction of one axis, and the second number indicates how far to travel in the direction of the second axis, with the convention that the names of the two axes and the coordinates correspond (e.g., x-axis and x-coordinate, y-axis and y-coordinate).
	5.G.2	Represent real world and mathematical problems by graphing points in the first quadrant of the coordinate plane, and interpret coordinate values of points in the context of the situation.
Instructional Days:	5	
Coherence		
Links from:	G4–M4	Angle Measure and Plane Figures
	G4–M5	Fraction Equivalence, Ordering, and Operations
Links to:	G6–M4	Expressions and Equations

Objective 1: Construct parallel line segments on a rectangular grid.
(Lesson 13)

Objective 2: Construct parallel line segments, and analyze relationships of the coordinate pairs.
(Lesson 14)

Objective 3: Construct perpendicular line segments on a rectangular grid.
(Lesson 15)

Objective 4: Construct perpendicular line segments, and analyze relationships of the coordinate pairs.
(Lesson 16)

Objective 5: Draw symmetric figures using distance and angle measure from the line of symmetry.
(Lesson 17)

Topic D: Problem Solving in the Coordinate Plane

Applications of the coordinate plane in the real world are the focus of Topic D. Students use the coordinate plane to show locations, movement, and distance on maps. Line graphs are also used to explore patterns in the coordinate plane and make predictions based on those patterns (5.G.2, 5.OA.3). To close their work with the coordinate plane, students solve real-world problems.

Focus Standard:	5.OA.3	Generate two numerical patterns using two given rules. Identify apparent relationships between corresponding terms. Form ordered pairs consisting of corresponding terms from the two patterns, and graph the ordered pairs on a coordinate plane. *For example, given the rule "Add 3" and the starting number 0, and given the rule "Add 6" and the starting number 0, generate terms in the resulting sequences, and observe that the terms in one sequence are twice the corresponding terms in the other sequence. Explain informally why this is so.*
	5.G.2	Represent real world and mathematical problems by graphing points in the first quadrant of the coordinate plane, and interpret coordinate values of points in the context of the situation.
Instructional Days:	3	
Coherence		
Links from:	G4–M4	Angle Measure and Plane Figures
Links to:	G6–M1	Ratios and Unit Rates

Objective 1: Draw symmetric figures on the coordinate plane.
(Lesson 18)

Objective 2: Plot data on line graphs and analyze trends.
(Lesson 19)

Objective 3: Use coordinate systems to solve real-world problems.
(Lesson 20)

Topic E: Multistep Word Problems

Topic E provides an opportunity for students to encounter complex, multistep problems requiring the application of the concepts and skills they mastered throughout the Grade 5 curriculum. Students use all four operations with both whole and fractional numbers in varied contexts. The problems in Topic E are designed to be nonroutine problems that require students to persevere in order to solve them.

While wrestling with complexity is an important part of Topic E, the true strength of this topic is derived from the time allocated for students to construct arguments and critique the reasoning of their classmates. After students have been given adequate time to ponder and solve the problems, two lessons are devoted to sharing approaches and solutions. Students partner to justify their conclusions, communicate them to others, and respond to the arguments of their peers.

Instructional Days:	5	
Coherence		
Links from:	G4–M1	Place Value, Rounding, and Algorithms for Addition and Subtraction
	G4–M3	Multi-Digit Multiplication and Division
	G4–M5	Fraction Equivalence, Ordering, and Operations
	G4–M6	Decimal Fractions
	G4–M7	Exploring Measurement with Multiplication
Links to:	G6–M1	Ratios and Unit Rates
	G6–M2	Arithmetic Operations Including Division of Fractions
	G6–M5	Area, Surface Area, and Volume Problems

Objective 1: Make sense of complex, multistep problems and persevere in solving them. Share and critique peer solutions.
(Lessons 21 through 25)

Topic F: The Year in Review: A Reflection on A Story of Units

In this final topic of Module 6, and in fact, the final topic of A *Story of Units*, students spend time producing a compendium of their learning. They not only reach back to recall learning from the very beginning of Grade 5 but also expand their thinking by exploring such concepts as the Fibonacci sequence. Students solidify the year's learning by creating and playing games and exploring patterns as they reflect back on their elementary years. All materials for the games and activities are then housed for summer use in boxes that students create in the final two lessons of the year.

Objective 1: Solidify writing and interpreting numerical expressions.
(Lessons 26 and 27)

Objective 2: Solidify fluency with Grade 5 skills.
(Lesson 28)

Objective 3: Solidify the vocabulary of geometry.
(Lessons 29 and 30)

Objective 4: Explore the Fibonacci sequence.
(Lesson 31)

Objective 5: Explore patterns in saving money.
(Lesson 32)

Objective 6: Design and construct boxes to house materials for summer use.
(Lessons 33 and 34)

CHAPTER 7

Mathematical Models

A *Story of Units* is a curriculum written by teachers for teachers to help every student build mastery of the new college- and career-ready standards. The theme of the story—creating, manipulating, and relating units—glues seemingly separate ideas into a coherent whole throughout each grade and over the years.

As noted in chapter 2, coherence is supported in *A Story of Units* through the use concrete and pictorial models. Students build increasing dexterity with these models through persistent use within and across levels of curriculum. The repeated appearance of familiar models helps to build vertical links between the topics of one grade level and the next. In addition, the depth of awareness that students have with the models not only ensures that they naturally become a part of the students' schema but also facilitates a more rapid and multifaceted understanding of new concepts as they are introduced.

This information is designed to support teachers as they engage students in meaningful mathematical learning experiences aligned to the standards. This support is provided through the following information:

- The grade levels for which the model is most appropriate

- A description and example of the model

- A collection of instructional strategies for using the model presented in order of the natural progression of the concepts

The following categories indicate the primary application area for each model. Of course, models appear repeatedly across grades and topics. Therefore, instructional strategies include examples spanning several levels of the curriculum.

Numbers through 10	Place Value and Standard Algorithms	Fractions
• Number Towers	• Bundles	• Number Line
• Number Path	• Place Value Chart	• Area Models
• Number Bond	• Base-Ten Blocks	
	• Money	
	• Number Disks (with Place Value Chart)	
Addition and Subtraction	**Multiplication**	**Word Problems**
• Ten-Frame	• Array and Area Models	• Tape Diagram
	• Rekenrek	

ARRAY AND AREA MODELS

GRADE LEVEL 1–5

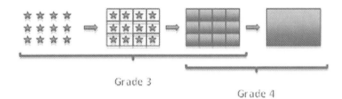

Grade 3

Grade 4

An array is an arrangement of a set of objects organized into equal groups in rows and columns. Arrays help make counting easy. Counting by equal groups is more efficient than counting objects one-by-one. The ten-frame is an array used in Kindergarten (see also the "Ten-Frame" section in this chapter). Students count objects in arrays in Kindergarten and PreKindergarten (PK.CC.4). The rectangular array is used to teach multiplication and leads to understanding area (3.OA.3).

Arrays reinforce the meaning of multiplication as repeated addition (e.g., $3 \times 4 = 4 + 4 + 4$) and the two meanings of division—that $12 \div 3$ can indicate how many will be in each group if I make 3 equal groups and that it can also indicate how many groups I can make if I put 3 in each group. Using arrays also reinforces the relationship between multiplication and division.

Instructional Strategies

- Use number towers to depict multiplication problems in the shape of an array (see also the "Number Towers" section in this chapter).

4   8   12   16

$4 \times 4 = \_\_\_.$
$16 \div 4 = \_\_.$

5 fours + 1 four = 6 fours
20 + 4 = 24
6×4 is 4 more than 5×4.

4   8   12   16   20   24

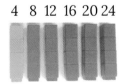

- Use the rectangular grid to model multiplication and division.

$4 \times 6 =$ ____.
$6 \times 4 =$ ____.

$4 \times$ ____ $= 24$.
____ $\times 6 = 24$.

$24 \div 4 =$ __.
$24 \div 6 =$ __.

- Multiply units with arrays.

  Multiplying hundreds:

4 hundreds $\times 3 = 12$ hundreds.
$400 \times 3 = 1,200$.

BASE-TEN BLOCKS

GRADE LEVEL K–2

Base-ten blocks (also referred to as *Dienes blocks*) include thousands "cubes," hundreds "flats," tens "rods," and ones "cubes." Base-ten blocks are a proportional representation of units of ones, tens, hundreds, and thousands and are useful for developing place value understanding. This is a "pregrouped" model for base-ten that allows efficient modeling of larger quantities through the thousands. However, because this place value model requires students to more abstractly consider the 10-to-1 relationship of the various blocks, care must be taken to ensure that they attend to the "ten-ness" of the pieces that are now traded rather than bundled or unbundled.

Base-ten blocks are introduced after students have learned the value of hundreds, tens, and ones and have had repeated experiences with composing and decomposing groups of 10 ones or groups of 10 tens with bundles.

INSTRUCTIONAL STRATEGIES

Instructional strategies for base-ten blocks are similar to those of bundles and place value disks. (See the "Bundles," "Money," and "Number Disks" sections for other teaching ideas.)

- Represent quantities on the mat, and write in standard, expanded, and word form.

- Play "more" and "less" games. Begin with an amount on a mat. At a predetermined signal (e.g., teacher claps or rings a bell), students add (or subtract) a quantity (2, 5, 10, or other) to (or from) the blocks on the mat.

- Give students equivalent representation riddles to be solved with base-ten pieces—for example, "I have 29 ones and 2 hundreds. What number am I?"

- Model addition, subtraction, multiplication, and division.

- Use blocks and mats as a support for teaching students to record the standard algorithms for all four operations.

BUNDLES

GRADE LEVEL K–2

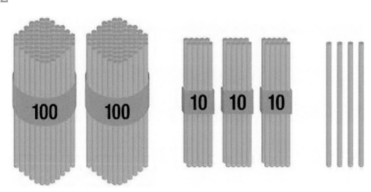

Bundles are discrete groupings of place value units (tens, hundreds, thousands), usually made by placing a rubber band or chenille stem around straws, popsicle sticks, or coffee stirrers. Linking cubes may also be used in this fashion. Ten straws (or cubes) are bundled (or linked) into 1 unit of ten, 10 tens are bundled into 1 unit of one hundred, and so on. These student-made groupings provide the necessary conceptual foundation for children to be successful with pregrouped, proportional, and nonproportional base-ten materials. (See also the "Base-Ten Blocks" and "Number Disks" sections in this chapter.)

Understanding tens and ones is supported in Kindergarten as students learn to compose and decompose tens and ones by bundling and unbundling the materials. Numbers 11 to 19 are soon seen as 1 ten (a bundled set of 10 ones) and some extra ones.

By Grade 2, students expand their skill with and understanding of units by bundling units of ones, tens, and hundreds up to one thousand with sticks. These larger units are discrete and can be counted: "1 hundred, 2 hundred, 3 hundred . . ." Bundles also help students extend their understanding of place value to 1,000 (2.NBT.1). Repeated bundling experiences help students to internalize the pattern that 10 of one unit make 1 of the next larger unit. Expanded form, increased understanding of skip counting (2.NBT.2), and fluency in counting larger numbers are all supported by the use of this model.

Bundles are also useful in developing conceptual understanding of renaming in addition and subtraction. The mat pictured here shows 2 tens and 3 ones. To solve 23 − 9, one bundle of ten is "unbundled" to get 1 ten and 13 ones in order to take away 9 ones.

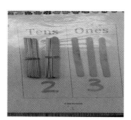

INSTRUCTIONAL STRATEGIES

- Represent various quantities with bundles and "singles."

- Count school days. Each day, a single straw or stick is added to the ones pocket and counted. Sticks are bundled when 10 days have passed and moved to the tens pocket. Have a "100th Day" celebration.

- Bundles may also be used to count down to a significant event (e.g., the last day of school), unbundling as necessary.

- Play Race to Zero with a partner. Students start with a quantity between 30 and 40 in bundles. Roll two dice to determine what can be taken away from the starting quantity (unbundling as necessary). The first partner to reach zero is the winner. This game may also be played as an addition game.

- Count in unit form (e.g., 2 tens, 8 ones; 2 tens, 9 ones; 3 tens).

- Represent quantities on place value mats to be added or subtracted.

MONEY

GRADE LEVEL 2

Dollar bills (1s, 10s, and 100s) are nonproportional units used to develop place value understanding. That is, bills are an abstract representation of place value because their value is not proportionate to their size. Ten bills can have a value of $10 or $1,000 but appear identical aside from their printed labels. Bills can be "traded" (e.g., 10 ten-dollar bills for 1 hundred-dollar bill) to help students learn the equivalence of the two amounts.

As with other place value models, students can use bills to model numbers up to three digits, read numbers formed with the bills, and increase fluency in skip-counting by tens and hundreds.

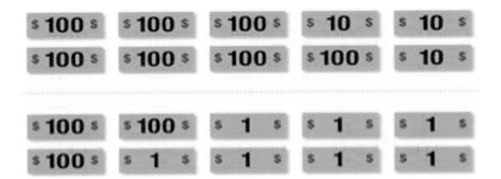

The picture shows that the arrangement of the $100s, $10s, and $1s can be counted in this manner:

For the first frame, the student might say, "100, 200, 300, 400, 500, 600, 700, 710, 720, 730."

For the second frame, the student might say, "100, 200, 300, 301, 302, 303, 304, 305, 306, 307."

The transition from a discrete unit of a bundle to proportional materials, such as base-ten blocks to a nonproportional unit of a bill, is a significant leap in a student's place value learning trajectory.

INSTRUCTIONAL STRATEGIES

- Skip-count up and down by $10 between 45 and 125: "45, 55, 65, 75, 85, 95, 105, 115, 125."
- Practice "making change" by counting on from a starting amount up to a specified total.
- "More" and "Less" games may also be played with money. (See also the "Base-Ten Blocks" section in this chapter.)
- Play equivalency games. "How many $5 bills in a $10 bill? A $20 bill? A $100 bill?"

NUMBER BOND

GRADE LEVEL K–5

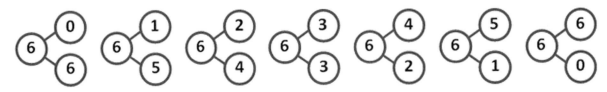

The number bond is a pictorial representation of part-part-whole relationships and shows that, within a part-whole relationship, smaller numbers (the parts) make up larger numbers (the whole). The number bond may be presented as shown in the picture, using smaller circles (or squares) for the parts to distinguish the part from the whole. Number bonds may be presented using the same size shape for parts and whole as students become more comfortable using them.

Number bonds of 10 have the greatest priority because students will use them for adding and subtracting across 10. Students move toward fluency in Grade 1 with numbers to 10 building on the foundation laid in Kindergarten. They learn to decompose numbers to 10 with increasing fluency (1.OA.6). Students learn the meaning of addition as "putting together" to find the whole or total and subtraction as "taking away" to find a part.

Notice in the diagram that the orientation of the number bond does not change its meaning and function ($6+2=8$, $2+6=8$, $8-6=2$, $8-2=6$).

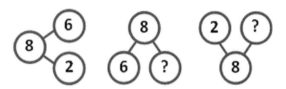

INSTRUCTIONAL STRATEGIES

- Make bonds with a specified whole using concrete objects. Students place all the objects into the "parts" circles of the bond using various combinations. The students can record them pictorially (drawing objects in the bonds), abstractly (writing numerals in the bonds), or using a combination of these representations as appropriate.

- Generate number stories for each number from 5 to 10 from pictures and situations.

- Develop fluency: Show all the possible ways to make ___, for all the numbers from 1 to 10.

- Present bonds in which the whole and one part are visible (using concrete, pictorial, and eventually abstract representations). Students solve for the other part by bonding, counting on, or subtracting.

- Transition students from number bonds to tape diagrams by drawing both representations for number stories.

- Use number bonds as a support for mental math techniques such as "make 10" (grade-specific examples follow).

- Use number bonds to see part-whole fraction and decimal relationships.

Grade 1 Example

Decompose 13 into 10 and 3.

Subtract 9 from the 10.

$$10-9=1$$

Then, add $1+3$.

$$1+3=4, \text{ so } 13-9=4.$$

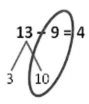

Grade 2 Example

Solve 24 + 33 mentally.
Use bonds to show your thinking.

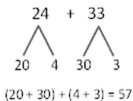

$(20 + 30) + (4 + 3) = 57$

Grade 4 Example 1

Decompose $\frac{4}{7}$ into $\frac{2}{7}$ and $\frac{2}{7}$.

Add $\frac{2}{7}$ to $\frac{5}{7}$ to make 1 whole.

$$\frac{2}{7} + \frac{5}{7} = \frac{7}{7}$$

Then, add $\frac{7}{7}$ to $\frac{2}{7}$.

$$\frac{7}{7} + \frac{2}{7} = \frac{9}{7} \text{ or } 1\frac{2}{7}$$

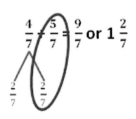

Grade 4 Example 2

T: 98 + 5 = 100 + _____?
S: 98 + 2 + 3 = 100 + 3.
T: 98 + 5 is _____?
S: 103.

98 + 5 = 103

T: 198 + 54 = 200 + _____?
S: 198 + 54 = 200 + 52.
T: 198 + 54 is _____?
S: 252.

198 + 54 = 152

T: 398 + 526 = 400 + _____?
S: 398 + 2 + 524 = 400 + 524.
T: 398 + 526 is _____?
S: 924.

398 + 526 = 924

NUMBER DISKS

GRADE LEVEL 2–5

Number disks are nonproportional units used to further develop place value understanding. Like money, the value of the disk is determined by the value printed on it, not by its size. Students through Grade 5 use number disks when modeling algorithms and as a support for mental math with very large whole numbers. Whole number place value relationships modeled with the disks are easily generalized to decimal numbers and operations with decimals.

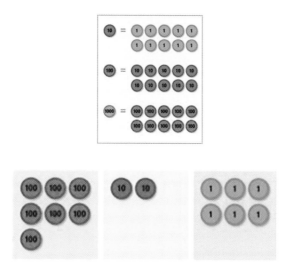

Place Value Chart with Number Disks

INSTRUCTIONAL STRATEGIES

- Play pattern games—for example: "What is 100 less than 253?" Students simply remove a 100 disk and state or record their new number.

- Play partner games. Partner A hides the disks from partner B within a file folder. Partner A says, "I am looking at the number 241. I will make 10 less [physically removing a 10 disk]. What is 10 less than 241?" Partner B writes the answer on his or her personal board or notebook and then states a full response: "Ten less than 241 is 231." Partner A removes the folder, and the partners compare the written response with the disks.

- Perform all four operations with both whole numbers and decimals on mats.

- Use materials to bridge to recording the standard algorithms for all four operations with both whole numbers and decimals.

NUMBER LINE

GRADE LEVEL K–5

The number line is used to develop a deeper understanding of whole number units, fraction units, measurement units, decimals, and negative numbers. Throughout Grades K–5, the number line models measuring units.

INSTRUCTIONAL STRATEGIES

- Measure lengths in meters and centimeters.

- Counting on: Have students place their finger on the location for the first addend, and count from there to add the second addend.

- Have students use a "clock" made from a 24-inch ribbon marked off at every 2 inches to skip-count by fives.

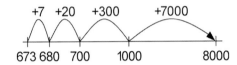

- Compute differences by counting up:

$$8,000 - 673 = 7,327$$

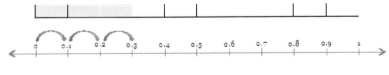

- Multiplying by 10: students visualize how much 5 tens is, and relate it to the number line.

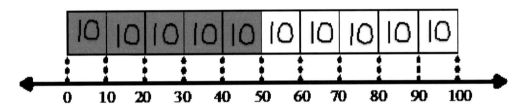

- Rounding to the nearest ten or hundred: students identify which hundreds come before 820: "820 is between 800 and 900."

- Model tenths in unit, expanded, fraction, and decimal form.

$$3 \text{ tenths} \ = \ 3 \times \frac{1}{10} \ = \ \frac{3}{10} \ = \ 0.3$$

- Create and analyze line plots.

NUMBER PATH

GRADE LEVEL PREK–1

1	2	3	4	5	6	7	8	9	10

The number path can be thought of as a visual (pictorial) representation of the number tower (see the "Number Towers" section in this chapter) and is foundational to understanding and using the number line. It also serves as a visual representation of 1:1 correspondence and the concept of whole numbers (one number, one space, and each being equal in size). The color change at 5 helps to reinforce the 5 and 10 benchmarks. The number path also serves as an early precursor to measurement concepts and a support for cardinal counting. (If a student places 7 objects in each of the 7 spaces on the path, he or she must realize that there are 7 objects, not 10. Simply because the path goes up to 10 does not mean there are 10 objects.)

INSTRUCTIONAL STRATEGIES

- Sort, classify, and count up to 5 with meaning, and then work on extending "how many" questions up to 10.

- Match amounts to numerals.

- Write numerals 1 to 5.

- Extend the meaning of 6, 7, and 8 with numerals (6 is 5 and 1; 7 is 5 and 2; 8 is 5 and 3).

- Become fluent with numbers to 10 and practice "before" and "after," as well as relationships of "1 more/less" and "2 more/less"

- Order numbers from 1 to 10.

- Play number order games—for example, partner A closes eyes while partner B covers a number in a number line with a penny; then partner A opens eyes and says the hidden number.

- Fold the number path so that only small sections are visible. Students show 4, 5, 6, 7; the teacher says, "4, 5, hmm, 7. What number is missing?"

- Play I Wish I Had games—for example, "I wish I had 7, but I have only 5." The student answers by placing a finger on 5 and then counting on to say "2"—the amount needed to make the target number.

- Match ordered sets with numerals on the number path.

NUMBER TOWERS

GRADE LEVEL PREK–3

Number towers, also known as number stairs, are representations of quantity constructed by joining together interlocking cubes. At the beginning of *A Story of Units*, these cubes are used to help younger children quite literally build their knowledge of cardinality by erecting towers of various numbers. Number towers are then used to teach concepts of more/less globally and the patterns of 1 more/less and 2 more/less specifically. This model leads to an understanding of comparison and the word *than*, not only in the context of "more than" and "less than," but also in the context of "taller than," "shorter than," heavier than," "longer than," and so on.

Children are encouraged to build towers for quantities 1 through 5 in one color. For quantities beyond 5, they add on in a second color. This color change provides support for several important developmental milestones. First, it facilitates children's understanding of 5 as a benchmark, which provides an important beginning to their ability to subitize ("instantly see how many"). Second, it allows students to see relationships such as "5 needs 2 more to be 7," "5 is 1 less than 6," and "5 and 4 is 9, which is 1 less than 10." Finally, it encourages students to count on from 5 rather than starting at 1 to count quantities of 6, 7, 8, 9, and 10.

Such comparisons lead to looking at the parts that make up a number ("3 is less than 7; 3 and 4 make 7"). These concepts are foundational to students' understanding of part/whole models (see also the "Number Bond" section in this chapter). This understanding leads naturally to discussions of addition and subtraction, fact fluencies (+1, +2, +3, -1, -2, -3), and even the commutative property ("Flip the tower; 3 + 4 or 4 + 3. Does the whole change?"), which are explored in Kindergarten and Grade 1.

In Grades 2 and 3, as students prepare for and study multiplication and division, each unit in the number stair can be ascribed a value other than 1—for example, "Each of our cubes is equal to 3. What is the value of the stair with 5 cubes?"

3 3 3 3 3

The use of number stairs can be extended to help children understand more complex properties like the distributive property: "Each of our cubes is equal to three. Make a stair with 5 cubes. Now, add 2 more cubes. The stair with 7 cubes is 2 more threes. So, 5 threes is 15, 2 threes is 6, and together 7 threes is 15+6 or 21."

$$5\text{ threes} + 2\text{ threes} = (5+2)\text{ threes}$$

INSTRUCTIONAL STRATEGIES

- Sort, classify, and count up to 5 with meaning, and then begin extending "how many" questions up to 10.

- Build a series of towers from 1 to 10, and then use the towers to relate quantities—for example, "5 is before 6," "6 is after 5," "5+1 more is 6," "6 is more than 5," "6 is 1 more than 5," "5 is 1 less than 6," "5 and 2 make 7," and "5+2=7."

- Build a tower that shows 6.

- Build a specific tower and count the cubes (cardinality).

- Partners roll dice. Then, each partner builds a different tower and states which has more (less).

- Build a tower while stating the "1 more" relationship (e.g., "4; 1 more is 5").

- Deconstruct the tower while stating the "1 less" relationship (e.g., "7, 1 less is 6").

- Count on from 5 (e.g., to count 7, students use the color change to say "5, 6, 7" instead of starting from 1). The color change at 5 may be presented to students as a shortcut by having students slide their finger over a group of 5 as they count (subitizing).

- Count up from numbers other than 0 and 1.

- Count down from numbers other than 10 to numbers other than 0 and 1.

- Compare numbers within 1 and 10.

PLACE VALUE CHART

GRADE LEVEL 2–5

The place value chart is a graphic organizer that students can use (beginning in Grade 1 with tens and ones through Grade 5 with decimals) to see the coherence of place value and operations between different units.

The place value chart without headings is used with labeled materials such as disks:

Place Value Chart without Headings

The place value chart with headings is used with unlabeled materials such as base-ten blocks or bundles:

Place Value Chart with Headings

Hundreds	Tens	Ones

INSTRUCTIONAL STRATEGIES

- Have students build numbers on mats. Place value cards (aka hide zero cards) may be used to show the expanded form of a number that is represented on the place value chart.
- Count the total value of ones, tens, and hundreds with any discrete proportional or nonproportional material such as bundles, base-ten blocks, or number disks.

 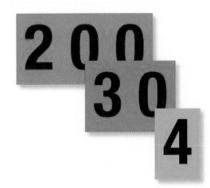

- Model and use language to tell about 1 more/less, 10 more/less on the place value chart with disks when there is change in the hundreds unit.
- Complete a pattern counting up and down.
- Model addition and subtraction using base-ten blocks or number disks.
- Use the mat and place value materials as a support for learning to record the standard algorithms for addition, subtraction, multiplication, and division.

REKENREK

GRADE LEVEL PREK–5

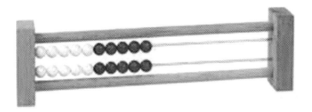

20-Bead Rekenrek

100-Bead Rekenrek

The Rekenrek has a 5 and 10 structure, with a color change at 5 (eliciting the visual effect of grouping 5 and grouping 10). The 20-bead Rekenrek consists of 2 rows of 10 beads, allowing students to see numbers to 10 as a number line on one row or a ten-frame (5 beads on two rows). A 100-bead Rekenrek has 10 rows of 10 beads. Other names for the Rekenrek are *calculating frame*, *Slavonic abacus*, *arithmetic rack*, and *math rack*.

INSTRUCTIONAL STRATEGIES

Grades PreK–1

- Count up and down in short sequences (1, 2, 3, 2, 3, 4, 3, 2, . . ., simulating the motion of a roller-coaster).
- Think of 7 as "2 more than 5."
- See "inside" numbers.
- Count in unit form (1 ten 1, 1 ten 2, 1 ten 3, . . . , 2 tens 1, 2 tens 2, and so on).
- Skip-count with complexity, such as counting by 10s on the 1s (3, 23, 33, 43, . . .).
- Group numbers in 5s and 10s. Compare the Rekenrek to the ten-frame.
- Build fluency with doubles.
- Make 10.
- Add across 10; subtract from 10.
- Build numbers 11 to 20.

- Show different strategies for adding $7+8$ ($5+5+2+3$, $7+7+1$, $10+5$, $8+8-1$).
- Compose and decompose numbers.
- Solve addition and subtraction story problems (e.g., putting together, taking away, part-part-whole and comparison).

Grades 2–5

- Show fluency with addition and subtraction facts.
- Find complements of numbers up to 10, 20, 30, . . . , 100.
- Skip count by 2, 3, 4, 5, 6, 7, 8, and 9 within 100.
- Identify doubles plus one and doubles minus one.
- Model rectangular arrays to build conceptual understanding of multiplication.
- Demonstrate the distributive property. Think of 3×12 as 3×10 plus 3×2.

TAPE DIAGRAM

GRADE LEVEL 1–5

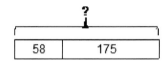

Rachel collected 58 seashells. Sam gave her 175 more. How many seashells did she have then?

Tape diagrams, also called *bar models*, are pictorial representations of relationships between quantities used to solve word problems. Students begin using tape diagrams in Grade 1, modeling simple word problems involving addition and subtraction. It is common for students in Grade 3 to say that they no longer need the tape diagram to solve the problem. However, in Grades 4 and 5, students begin to appreciate the tape diagram because it enables them to solve increasingly more complex problems.

At the heart of a tape diagram is the idea of *forming units*. In fact, forming units to solve word problems is one of the most powerful examples of the unit theme and is particularly helpful for understanding fraction arithmetic.

The tape diagram provides an essential bridge to algebra and is often called *pictorial algebra*.

Like any other tool, it is best introduced with simple examples and in small, managable steps so that students have time to reflect on the relationships they are drawing. For most students, structure is important. RDW, or Read, Draw, Write, is a simple process used for problem solving and is applicable to all grades:

1. Read.
2. Draw and label.

3. Write a number sentence.

4. Write a word sentence (statement).

The more students participate in reasoning through problems with a systematic approach, the more they internalize those behaviors and thought processes. What can I see? Can I draw something? What conclusions can I make from my drawing?

There are two basic forms of the tape diagram model. The first form, sometimes called the *part-whole model*, uses bar segments placed end-to-end (the Grade 3 example that follows depicts this model). The second form, sometimes called the comparison model, uses two or more bars stacked in rows that are typically left justified (the Grade 5 example that follows depicts this model).

Rather than talk to students about the two forms, simply model the more suitable form for a given problem and allow flexibility in the students' modeling. Over time, students will develop their own intuition for which model will work better for a given problem. It is helpful to ask students as a class, "Did anyone do it differently?" so they can see more than one way to model the problem. Then, perhaps ask, "Which way makes it easier for you to visualize this problem?"

Grade 3 Example

Priya baked 256 cookies. She sold some of them. 187 were left. How many did she sell?

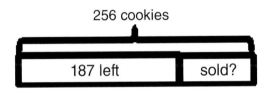

256 − 187 = ___

Priya sold <u>69</u> cookies.

Grade 5 Example

Sam has 1,025 animal stickers. He has 3 times as many plant stickers as animal stickers. How many plant stickers does Sam have? How many stickers does Sam have altogether?

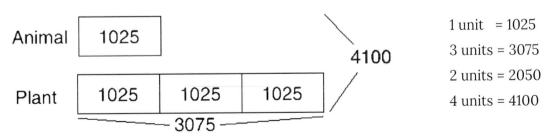

1. He has <u>3,075</u> plant stickers.

2. He has <u>4,100</u> stickers altogether.

INSTRUCTIONAL STRATEGIES

- Modeling two discrete quantities with small individual bars where each individual bar represents one unit. (This serves as an initial transition from the Unifix cube model to a pictorial version.)

Bobby's candy bars:

Molly's candy bars:

- Modeling two discrete quantities with incremented bars where each increment represents 1 unit:

Bobby's candy bars

Molly's candy bars

- Modeling two quantities (discrete or continuous) with nonincremented bars:

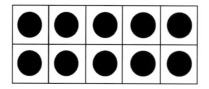

Bobby's candy bars

Molly's candy bars

- Modeling a part-part-whole relationship where the bars represent known quantities, the total is unknown.

- Modeling a part-part-whole relationship with one part unknown.

- Modeling addition and subtraction comparisons.

- Modeling with equal parts in multiplication and division problems.

- Modeling with equal parts in fraction problems.

TEN-FRAME

GRADE LEVEL PREK–3

A ten-frame is a 2-by 5-grid (array) used to develop an understanding of concepts such as 5-patterns, combinations to 10, and adding and subtracting within 20. The frame is filled beginning on the top row, left to right, then proceeding to the bottom row, building left to right. This pattern of filling supports subitizing by building on the 5 benchmark, as well as providing a pattern for placing disks on place value mats in later grades. Concrete counters, as well as pictorial dots, may be used to represent quantities on the frame.

In Kindergarten and early in Grade 1, a double ten-frame can be used to establish early foundations of place value (e.g., 13 is 10 and 3 or 1 ten and 3 ones). It can also be used on place value mats to support learning to add double-digit numbers with regrouping. The "completion of a unit" on the ten-frame in early grades empowers students in later grades to understand a "make 100 (or 1,000)" strategy, to add 298 and 37 (i.e., 298 + 2 + 35), and to more fully understand addition and subtraction of measurements (e.g., 4 ft 8 in + 5 in).

INSTRUCTIONAL STRATEGIES

- Flash a ten-frame for 3 to 5 seconds, and then ask students to recreate what was filled/not filled on their own personal ten-frame. (Students may also tell how many they saw or match the flash with a numeral card.)

- Use the flash technique, but ask students to tell 1 more or less than the number flashed.

- Roll dice and build the number on the ten-frame.

- Partner games: Partner A rolls a die and builds the number on the frame. Partner B rolls and adds that number to the frame (encouraging "10" and "leftovers" or using two ten-frames to represent the sum).

- Play Crazy Mixed-Up Numbers. Have children represent a number on the ten-frame. Then, give various directions for changing the frame (e.g., start with 4: "2 more," "1 less," "1 fewer," "double it," "take away 3"). This activity has the added benefit of providing the teacher with the opportunity to observe how students count—who clears the mat and starts over each time and who is counting on and/or subtracting.

- Write number stories about the filled and "unfilled" parts of the ten-frame.

- Counting in unit form:

Regular	Unit Form
Eleven	1 ten one
Twelve	1 ten two
Thirteen	1 ten three
Twenty	2 tens
Twenty-six	2 tens six

- Represent a number between 5 and 10 on the frame with one color counter. Have students add a quantity between 6 and 9, represented by a second color, to it (e.g., 7 + 6). Encourage students to "fill the frame" and restate the problem as 10 + 3.

CHAPTER 8

Terminology

The terms listed in this chapter were compiled from the New or Recently Introduced Terms portion of the Terminology section of the Module Overviews in *A Story of Units*. All grade levels are represented, from Prekindergarten to Grade 5. This list serves as a reference for teachers to quickly determine at which point in the curriculum terms are introduced. We provide descriptions, examples, and illustrations. It should be noted that, especially during the early years of learning, students are often spared exposure to formal definitions of terms due to their complexity.

GRADE PREK

Module 1

- 1 less (e.g., 1 less than 4 is 3)
- 1 more (e.g., 1 more than 4 is 5)
- After (position word)
- Count (with reference to use of number core)
- Counting the Math Way (count fingers from left pinky to right pinky)
- Different (way to analyze objects to match or sort)
- Exactly the same (way to analyze objects to match or sort)
- Group (objects sharing one or more attributes)
- How many (with reference to counting quantities or sets)
- Line (with reference to counting configuration)
- Mark (with reference to starting point for count)
- Match (group items that are the same or have the same given attribute)

- Number (numeral)
- Partners (embedded numbers)
- The same, but . . . (way to analyze objects to match or sort)
- Size (generalized measurement term)
- Sort (group objects according to a particular attribute)

Module 2

- Above, behind, below, between, down, in, in front of, next to, off, on, under, up (position words)
- Circle (two-dimensional shape whose boundary consists of points equidistant from the center)
- Corner (where two sides meet)
- Face (flat side of a solid)
- Flat (as opposed to round)
- Model (a representation of something)
- Pointy (having a sharp point)
- Rectangle (two-dimensional shape enclosed by four straight sides)
- Roll (attribute of a shape)
- Round (circular; shaped like a circle, sphere, cylinder)
- Shape (external boundary of an object)
- Side (position or with reference to a shape)
- Slide (attribute of a shape)
- Square (two-dimensional shape enclosed by four straight, equal sides)
- Stack (attribute of a shape)
- Straight (without a curve or bend)
- Triangle (two-dimensional shape enclosed by three straight sides)

Module 3

- 0, 6, 7, 8, 9, 10 (numerals)
- Shapes (rectangle, triangle, square, circle)
- Sides
- Tally marks
- Zero

Module 4

- About the same length/height/weight as (way to compare measurable attributes)
- Are there enough . . . ? (comparative question)

- Balance scale (tool for weight and measurement)
- Bigger than (volume or size comparison)
- Compare (specifically using direct comparison)
- Empty (volume comparison)
- Equal to (e.g., 5 is *equal to* 5.)
- Exactly enough/not enough (comparative term)
- Extra (leftovers)
- Fewer/fewer than (way to compare number of objects, e.g., "There are fewer apples than oranges.")
- First (comparing numbers related to order or position)
- Full (volume comparison)
- Greater/greater than (number comparison)
- Heavy/heavier/heavier than (weight comparison)
- Height (measurable attribute of objects, described as tall or short)
- Last (comparing numbers related to order or position)
- Length (measurable attribute of objects, described as long or short)
- Less than (with reference to volume, numbers of objects, or numbers, e.g., 3 is *less than* 4.)
- Light/lighter/lighter than (weight comparison)
- Long/longer/longer than (length comparison)
- More than (with reference to volume and numbers of objects)
- Same (with reference to volume, holding the same amount)
- Set (group of objects)
- Short/shorter/shorter than (length comparison)
- Smaller than (volume or size comparison)
- Tall/taller than (height comparison)
- Weigh/weight (measurable attribute of objects, described as heavy or light)

Module 5
- Add/addition
- Addition story
- All together
- Are left
- Equals
- In all
- Math drawing
- Number sentence

- Pattern
- Plus
- Put together
- Repeating part
- Sixteen, seventeen, eighteen, nineteen, twenty (number words)
- Subtract/subtraction
- Subtraction story
- Take away
- Total

GRADE K

Module 1

- 1 less (e.g., 4: 1 less is 3)
- 1 more (e.g., 4: 1 more is 5)
- 5-group (pictured)
- Counting path (with reference to order of count)
- Exactly the same/not exactly the same/the same, but . . . (ways to analyze objects to match or sort)
- Hidden partners (embedded numbers)
- How many (with reference to counting quantities or sets)
- Match (group items that are the same or have the same given attribute)
- Number path (pictured)
- Number sentence (e.g., 3 = 2 + 1)
- Number story (stories with *add to* or *take from* situations)
- Rows/columns (often used in reference to horizontal/vertical groups in a rectangular array)
- Sort (group objects according to a particular attribute)
- Zero

Module 2

- Above, below, beside, in front of, next to, behind (position words)
- Circle
- Cone (three-dimensional shape)
- Cube (three-dimensional shape)
- Cylinder (three-dimensional shape)
- Face (flat side of a solid)

- Flat (two-dimensional shape)
- Hexagon (flat illustration enclosed by six straight sides)
- Rectangle (flat illustration enclosed by four straight sides)
- Solid (three-dimensional shape)
- Sphere (three-dimensional shape)
- Square (flat illustration enclosed by four straight, equal sides)
- Triangle (flat illustration enclosed by three straight sides)

Module 3

- Balance scale (tool for weight measurement)
- Capacity (with reference to volume)
- Compare (specifically using direct comparison)
- Endpoint (with reference to alignment for direct comparison)
- Enough/not enough (comparative term)
- Heavier than/lighter than (weight comparison)
- Height (vertical distance measurement from bottom to top)
- Length (distance measurement from end to end; in a rectangular shape, length can be used to describe any of the four sides)
- Longer than/shorter than (length comparison)
- More than/fewer than (discrete quantity comparison)
- More than/less than (volume, area, and number comparisons)
- Taller than/shorter than (height comparison)
- The same as (comparative term)
- Weight

Module 4

- Addition (specifically using *add to with result unknown, put together with total unknown, put together with both addends unknown*)
- Addition and subtraction sentences (equations)
- Make 10 (combine two numbers from 1 to 9 that add up to 10)
- Minus (−)
- Number bond (mathematical model; pictured)
- Number pairs or partners (embedded numbers)
- Part (when used in the context of number–an addend or embedded number)
- Put together (add)
- Subtraction (specifically using *take from with result unknown*)

- Take apart (decompose)
- Take away (subtract)
- Whole (total)

Module 5

- 10 and ____
- 10 ones and some ones
- 10 plus
- Hide zero cards (in later grades, called place value cards; pictured)
- Regular counting by ones from 11 to 20 (e.g., 11, 12, 13, . . .)
- Regular counting by tens to 100 (e.g., 10, 20, 30, 40, 50, 60, 70, 80, 90, 100)
- Say ten counting by tens to 100 (e.g., 1 ten, 2 tens, 3 tens, 4 tens, 5 tens, 6 tens, 7 tens, 8 tens, 9 tens, 10 tens)
- Teen numbers

Module 6

- First, second, third, fourth, fifth, sixth, seventh, eighth, ninth, tenth (ordinal numbers)

GRADE 1

Module 1

- Addend (one of the numbers being added)
- Count on (students count up from one addend to the total)
- Doubles (e.g., 3 + 3 or 4 + 4)
- Doubles plus 1 (e.g., 3 + 4 or 4 + 5)
- Expression (e.g., 3 + 2, 7 − 1 as opposed to a number sentence, e.g., 3 + 2 = 5, 6 = 7 − 1)
- Track (students use different objects to track the count on from one addend to the total)

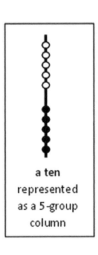

a ten represented as a 5-group column

Module 2

- A ten (pictured)
- Ones (basic units of the place value system, 10 ones = 1 ten)

Module 3

- Centimeter (standard length unit within the metric system)
- Centimeter cube (pictured)
- Length unit (e.g., centimeters, inches)

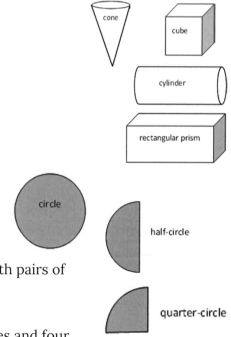

Module 4

- \> (greater than)
- < (less than)
- Place value (the unit associated with a particular digit due to its position within a number; also used in reference to the place value system)

Module 5

- Attributes (characteristics of an object, such as color or number of sides)
- Fourth of (shapes), fourths (1 out of 4 equal parts)
- Half of, halves (shapes)
- Half past (expression for 30 minutes past a given hour)
- Half-hour (interval of time lasting 30 minutes)
- Hour (unit for measuring time, equivalent to 60 minutes or 1/24 of a day)
- Minute (unit for measuring time, equivalent to 60 seconds, 1/60 of an hour)
- O'clock (used to indicate time to a precise hour, with no additional minutes)
- Quarter of (shapes) (1 out of 4 equal parts)
- Three-dimensional shapes:
  - Cone (pictured)
  - Cube (pictured)
  - Cylinder (pictured)
  - Rectangular prism (pictured)
  - Sphere
- Two-dimensional shapes:
  - Circle (pictured)
  - Half-circle (pictured)
  - Hexagon (flat shape enclosed by six straight sides)
  - Parallelogram (a flat, four-sided shape in which both pairs of opposite sides are parallel)
  - Quarter-circle (pictured)
  - Rectangle (flat shape enclosed by four straight sides and four right angles)
  - Rhombus (flat shape enclosed by four straight sides of the same length)

- Square (a rectangle with all sides of equal length—viewed as a "special rectangle")
- Trapezoid (pictured)
- Triangle (flat illustration enclosed by three straight sides)

trapezoid

Module 6

- Comparison problem type
- Dime
- Nickel
- Penny
- Quarter

GRADE 2

Module 1

No new or recently introduced terms

Module 2

- Benchmark (e.g., "round" numbers like multiples of 10)
- Endpoint (e.g., the point where something begins or ends)
- Estimate (an approximation of a quantity or number)
- Hash mark (the marks on a ruler or other measurement tool)
- Meter (m, a standard unit of length in the metric system)
- Meter stick
- Meter strip (pictured)
- Number line (pictured)
- Overlap (extend over, or cover partly)
- Ruler (tool used to measure length)

Module 3

- Base-ten numerals (e.g., a thousand is 10 hundreds, a hundred is 10 tens; starting in Grade 3, a one is 10 tenths, and so on)
- Expanded form (e.g., 500 + 70 + 6)
- Hundreds place (e.g., the 5 in 576 is in the hundreds place)

- One thousand (1,000)
- Place value or number disk (pictured)
- Place value chart (pictured)
- Standard form (e.g., 576)
- Word form (e.g., five hundred seventy-six)

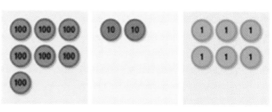

Say Ten form modeled with number disks:
7 hundreds 2 tens 6 ones = 72 tens 6 ones

Module 4

- Equation (a statement that two expressions are equal, e.g., $3 \times \underline{\quad} = 12$, $7 = 21 \div b$, $5 \times 4 = 20$. Note that, while an equation may or may not contain an unknown number, once the unknowns are filled in, one is left with a number sentence.)
- Minuend (e.g., the 9 in $9 - 6 = 3$)
- New groups below (pictured)
- Number sentence (an equation or inequality for which both expressions are numerical (can be evaluated to a single number)—for example, $4 \times 3 = 6 \times 2$, $21 > 7 \times 2$, $5 \div 5 = 1$. Number sentences are either true or false— for example, $4 \times 4 < 6 \times 2$ and $21 = 7 \times 4$—and contain no unknowns.
- Subtrahend (e.g., the 6 in $9 - 6 = 3$)
- Totals below (pictured)

Place Value Chart with Headings
(use with numbers)

hundreds	tens	ones
7	2	6

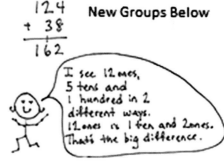

New Groups Below

I see 12 ones, 5 tens and 1 hundred in 2 different ways. 12 ones is 1 ten and 2 ones. That's the big difference.

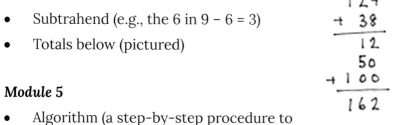

Totals Below

Module 5

- Algorithm (a step-by-step procedure to solve a particular type of problem)
- Compensation (simplifying strategy where students add or subtract the same amount to or from both numbers to create an equivalent but easier problem)
- Compose (e.g., to make 1 larger unit from 10 smaller units)
- Decompose (e.g., to break 1 larger unit into 10 smaller units)
- Simplifying strategy (e.g., to solve $299 + 6$, think $299 + 1 + 5 = 300 + 5 = 305$)

Module 6

- Array (e.g., an arrangement of objects in rows and columns)
- Columns (the vertical groups in a rectangular array)
- Even number (e.g., a whole number whose last digit is 0, 2, 4, 6, or 8)
- Odd number (any number that is not even)

- Repeated addition (e.g., 2 + 2 + 2)
- Rows (the horizontal groups in a rectangular array)
- Tessellation (tiling of a plane using one or more geometric shapes with no overlaps and no gaps)
- Whole number (e.g., 0, 1, 2, 3 . . .)

Module 7

- Bar graph (pictured)
- Category (group of people or things sharing a common characteristic, e.g., bananas are in the fruit category)
- Data (a set of facts or pieces of information)
- Degree (used to measure temperature, e.g., degrees Fahrenheit)
- Foot (ft, unit of length equal to 12 inches)
- Inch (in, unit of length)
- Legend (notation on a graph explaining what symbols represent)
- Line plot (graphical representation of data; pictured)
- Picture graph (representation of data like a bar graph, using pictures instead of bars; pictured)
- Scale (a number line used to indicate the various quantities represented in a bar graph; pictured)
- Survey (collecting data by asking a question and recording responses)
- Symbol (picture that represents something else)
- Table (representation of data using rows and columns)
- Thermometer (temperature measuring tool)
- Yard (yd, unit of length equal to 36 inches or 3 feet)

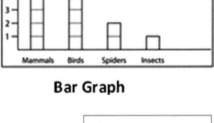

Bar Graph

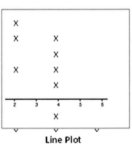

Line Plot

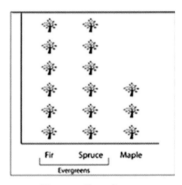

Picture Graph

Scale

Module 8

- a.m./p.m.
- Analog clock (pictured)
- Angle (e.g., illustration formed by the corner of a polygon)
- Digital clock
- Parallel (used to describe opposite sides of a parallelogram, e.g., "These sides are parallel, because if they kept on going, they'd never intersect!")
- Parallelogram (quadrilateral with both pairs of opposite sides parallel)

- Polygon (closed illustration with three or more straight sides, e.g., triangle, quadrilateral, pentagon, hexagon)
- Quadrilateral (four-sided polygon, e.g., square, rhombus, rectangle, parallelogram, trapezoid)
- Quarter past, quarter to
- Right angle (e.g., a square corner)
- Second (unit for measuring time, 60 seconds is equivalent to 1 minute and 1/60 of a minute)
- Third of (shapes), thirds (1 out of 3 equal parts)
- Trapezoid (a quadrilateral in which at least one pair of opposite sides is parallel)
- Whole (used in reference to fractions, e.g., 2 halves make 1 whole, 3 thirds make 1 whole)

GRADE 3

Module 1

- Commutative property/commutative (e.g., $3 \times 5 = 5 \times 3$)
- Distribute (with reference to the Distributive Property, e.g., in $12 \times 3 = (10 + 2) \times 3 = (10 \times 3) + (2 \times 3)$)
- Divide/division (e.g., $15 \div 5 = 3$, which is interpreted as either 15 divided into groups of 5 equals 3 or 15 divided into 5 groups equals 3)
- Equal groups
- Expression (a number, or any combination of sums, differences, products, or divisions of numbers that evaluates to a number, e.g., $3 + 4$, 8×3, $4 + b$, $3 \times 4 + 5 \times 4$ as distinct from an equation or number sentence; see Grade 2 Module 4)
- Fact (used to refer to multiplication facts, e.g., 3×2)
- Factors (numbers that are multiplied to obtain a product)
- Multiply/multiplication (e.g., $5 \times 3 = 15$, which is interpreted as 5 groups of 3 equals 15)
- Number of groups (factor in a multiplication problem that refers to the total number of equal groups)
- Parentheses ( ) (the symbols used around a fact or numbers within an equation)
- Quotient (the answer when one number is divided by another)
- Rotate (turn; used with reference to turning arrays 90 degrees)
- Row/column (in reference to rectangular arrays)
- Size of groups (factor in a multiplication problem that refers to how many in a group)
- Unit (used to refer to one part of a tape diagram partitioned into equal parts)
- Unknown (used to refer to the missing number in a number sentence)

Module 2

- About (with reference to rounding and estimation; used to indicate an answer that is not precise)
- Addend (e.g., in 4 + 5, the numbers 4 and 5 are the addends)
- Capacity (the amount of liquid that a particular container can hold)
- Continuous (with reference to time as a continuous measurement)
- Endpoint (used with rounding on the number line; the numbers that mark the beginning and end of a given interval)
- Gram (g, a unit of measurement for weight in the metric system)
- Halfway (with reference to a number line, the midpoint between two numbers, e.g., 5 is halfway between 0 and 10)
- Interval (e.g., an amount of time passed or a segment on the number line)
- Kilogram (kg, a measurement unit for mass—not distinguished from weight at this stage)
- Liquid volume (the space a liquid takes up)
- Liter (L, a unit of measurement for liquid volume)
- Milliliter (mL, unit of measurement for liquid volume)
- Plot (locate and label a point on a number line)
- Point (used to refer to a specific location on the number line)
- Reasonable (with reference to how plausible an answer is, e.g., "Is your answer reasonable?")
- Rename (regroup units, e.g., when solving with the standard algorithm)
- Round (estimate a number to the nearest 10 or 100 using place value)
- Standard algorithm (for addition and subtraction)
- ≈ (symbol used to show than an answer is approximate)

Module 3

- Multiple (specifically with reference to naming multiples of 9 and 10, e.g., 20, 30, 40)
- Multiplier (the factor representing the number of units)
- Product (the quantity resulting from multiplying two or more numbers together)

Module 4

- Area (the amount of two-dimensional space in a bounded region)
- Area model (a model for multiplication based on area; pictured)

Module 1 and Module 3   Module 4

- Square unit (a unit of area—specifically square centimeters, inches, feet, and meters)
- Tile (to cover a region without gaps or overlaps)
- Unit square (e.g., given a length unit, it is a 1 unit by 1 unit square)
- Whole number (the numbers: 0, 1, 2, 3, . . .)

Module 5

- Copies (refers to the number of unit fractions in 1 whole)
- Equal parts (parts with equal measurements)
- Equivalent fractions (fractions that name the same size or the same point on the number line)
- Fractional unit (half, third, fourth, and so on)
- Nonunit fraction (fractions with numerators other than 1)
- Unit fraction (fractions with numerator 1)
- Unit interval (the interval from 0 to 1)

Module 6

- Measurement data (e.g., length measurements of a collection of pencils)
- Most frequent (most common measurement on a line plot)
- Scaled graphs (bar or picture graph in which the scale uses units with a value greater than 1)
- Survey (collecting data by asking a question and recording responses)

Module 7

- Attribute (any characteristic of a shape, including properties and other defining characteristics, e.g., straight sides, and nondefining characteristics, e.g., blue)
- Diagonal (e.g., the line drawn between opposite corners of a quadrilateral)
- Perimeter (boundary or length of the boundary of a two-dimensional shape)
- Property (e.g., squares have the property that all sides are equal in length)
- Regular polygon (polygon whose side lengths and interior angles are all equal)
- Tessellate (to tile a plane without gaps or overlaps)
- Tetrominoes (four identical squares arranged to form a shape so that every square shares at least one side with another square)

GRADE 4

Module 1

- Algorithm
- One million, ten millions, hundred millions (as places on the place value chart)
- Ten thousands, hundred thousands (as places on the place value chart)

Module 2

- Kilometer (km, a unit of length measurement)
- Mass (a measurement of the amount of matter in an object—not distinguished from weight at this stage)
- Milliliter (mL, a unit of measurement for liquid volume)
- Mixed units (e.g., 3 m 43 cm)

Module 3

- Associative Property (e.g., $96 = 3 \times (4 \times 8) = (3 \times 4) \times 8$)
- Composite number (positive integer having three or more whole number factors)
- Distributive Property (e.g., $64 \times 27 = (60 \times 20) + (60 \times 7) + (4 \times 20) + (4 \times 7)$)
- Divisor (e.g., the 3 in $37 \div 3$)
- Partial product (e.g., in the calculation $24 \times 6 = (20 \times 6) + (4 \times 6) = 120 + 24$, 120 and 24 are partial products)
- Prime number (positive integer greater than 1 having whole number factors of only 1 and itself)
- Remainder (the number left over when one integer is divided by another)

Module 4

- Acute angle (angle that measures less than 90 degrees)
- Acute triangle (triangle with all interior angles measuring less than 90 degrees)
- Adjacent angle (e.g., ∠ADC and ∠CDB are called adjacent angles; pictured)

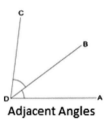
Adjacent Angles

- Angle (union of two noncollinear rays sharing a common vertex)
- Arc (connected portion of a circle; pictured)

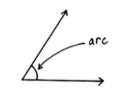
arc

- Collinear (three or more points are *collinear* if there is a line containing all of the points; otherwise, the points are *noncollinear*)
- Complementary angles (two angles with a sum of 90 degrees; pictured)
- Degree measure of an angle. (Subdivide the length around a circle into 360 arcs of equal length. A central angle for any of these arcs is called a *one-degree angle* and is said to have angle measure 1 degree.)

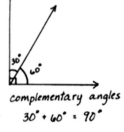
complementary angles
$30° + 60° = 90°$

- Diagonal (straight lines joining two opposite corners of a straight-sided shape)
- Equilateral triangle (triangle with three equal sides; pictured)
- Illustration (set of points in the plane)

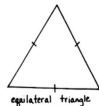
equilateral triangle

- Interior of an angle (pictured)

- Intersecting lines (lines that contain at least one point in common)

- Isosceles triangle (triangle with at least two equal sides; pictured)

- Length of an arc (circular distance around the arc)

- Line (straight path with no thickness that extends in both directions without end)

- Line of symmetry (line through an illustration such that when the illustration is folded along the line, two halves are created that match up exactly; pictured)

- Line segment (two points, A, B, together with the set of points on the line $\overline{AB}$ between A and B)

- Obtuse angle (angle with a measure greater than 90 degrees but less than 180 degrees)

- Obtuse triangle (triangle with an interior obtuse angle)

- Parallel (two lines that lie in the same plane and do not intersect)

- Perpendicular (two lines that intersect and any of the angles formed between the lines is a 90 degree angle.)

- Point (precise location in the plane)

- Protractor (instrument used in measuring or sketching angles)

- Ray. (The *ray* $\overrightarrow{OA}$ is the point O and the set of all points on the line $\overleftrightarrow{OA}$ that are on the same side of O as the point A)

- Right angle (an angle that measures 90 degrees, introduced earlier as "a square corner")

- Right triangle (triangle that contains one 90 degree angle)

- Scalene triangle (triangle with no equal sides)

- Straight angle (an "angle" that measures 180 degrees, i.e., a line)

- Supplementary angles (two angles whose measurements add up to 180 degrees; pictured)

- Triangle (consists of three noncollinear points and the three line segments between them; the three segments are the *sides* of the triangle, and the three points are the *vertices*)

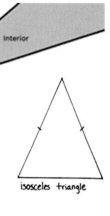

isosceles triangle

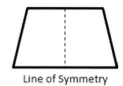

Line of Symmetry

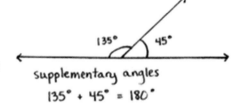

supplementary angles
135° + 45° = 180°

- Vertex (a point, often used to refer to the point where two lines meet, such as in an angle or the corner of a triangle)

- Vertical angles (when two lines intersect, any two nonadjacent angles formed by those lines; also called *vertically opposite angles*)

Module 5

- Benchmark fraction (e.g., $\frac{1}{2}$ is a benchmark fraction when comparing $\frac{1}{3}$ and $\frac{3}{5}$)

- Common denominator (when two or more fractions have the same denominator)

- Denominator (bottom number in a fraction)
- Like denominators (e.g., $\frac{1}{8}$ and $\frac{5}{8}$)
- Mixed number (e.g., $3\frac{1}{4}$, which is an abbreviated form for $3 \times \frac{1}{4}$)
- Numerator (top number in a fraction)
- Unlike denominators (e.g., $\frac{1}{8}$ and $\frac{1}{7}$)

Module 6

- Decimal expanded form (e.g., $(2 \times 10) + (4 \times 1) + (5 \times 0.1) + (9 \times 0.01) = 24.59$)
- Decimal fraction (fraction with a denominator of 10, 100, 1,000, and so on)
- Decimal number (number written using place value units of ones, tens, hundreds, and so on, as well as decimal fraction units, e.g., tenths, hundredths)
- Decimal point (period used to separate the whole number part from the fractional part of a decimal number)
- Fraction expanded form (e.g., $(2 \times 10) + (4 \times 1) + \left(5 \times \frac{1}{10}\right) + \left(9 \times \frac{1}{100}\right) = 24\frac{59}{100}$)
- Hundredth (place value unit such that 100 hundredths equals 1 one)
- Tenth (place value unit such that 10 tenths equals 1 one)

GRADE 5

Module 1

- Equation (two expressions with an equal sign between them, i.e., a statement that two expressions are equal, though without a guarantee that the statement is true)
- Exponents (e.g., $10^3 = 10 \times 10 \times 10$)
- Millimeter (mm, a metric unit of length equal to 1 thousandth of a meter)
- Thousandths (related to place value)

Module 2

- Multiplier (a quantity by which a given number is to be multiplied)
- Parentheses (the symbols used to indicate the order in which operations should be carried out)

Module 3

No new or recently introduced terms

Module 4

- Decimal divisor (the number that divides the whole and has units of tenths, hundredths, thousandths, and so on)
- Simplify (using the largest fractional unit possible to express an equivalent fraction)

Module 5

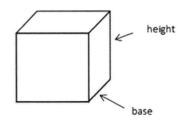

- Base (e.g., in a right rectangular prism, a choice of one face–often thought of as the face on which the prism rests; pictured)

- Bisect (divide into two equal parts)

- Cubic units (cubes of the same size used for measuring volume)

- Height (in a right rectangular prism, the length of an edge perpendicular to the chosen base; pictured)

- Hierarchy (pictured)

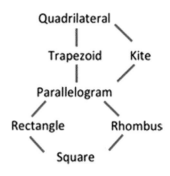

- Unit cube (cube whose sides all measure 1 unit; cubes of the same size used for measuring volume)

- Volume of a solid (measurement of space or capacity)

- Rectangle (a parallelogram having four right angles)

- Rhombus (a parallelogram in which all sides are of equal length)

- Kite (quadrilateral in which two adjacent sides have equal lengths and the remaining two sides also have equal but possibly different lengths)

Module 6

- Axis (fixed reference line used in the context of the coordinate plane)

- Coordinate (a number used to identify a location)

- Coordinate pair/ordered pair (two numbers that are used to identify a point on a plane; written (x, y) where x represents a distance from 0 on the x-axis and y represents a distance from 0 on the y-axis)

- Coordinate plane (a plane equipped with a coordinate system, and in which any point may be located by a coordinate pair)

- Origin (the point at which the x-axis and y-axis intersect, labeled (0, 0) on the coordinate plane)

- Quadrant (any of the four regions created by the intersection of the x-axis and y-axis)

Notes

CHAPTER 3

1. Multi-digit decimal multiplication such as 4.1 × 3.4 and division such as 4.5 ÷ 1.5 are studied in Module 4.

2. When a cluster is referred to in this chart without a footnote, the cluster is addressed in its entirety.

3. This standard is addressed again in Modules 2 and 4; the balance of this cluster is addressed in Module 2.

4. The focus of this module is on the metric system to reinforce place value and writing measurements using mixed units.

5. These skills are also applied to fractions in this module.

6. The balance of this cluster is addressed in Module 1.

7. From this point forward, fluency practice is part of the students' ongoing experience.

8. Focus on decimal multiplication of a single-digit, whole number factor times a multi-digit number with up to two decimal places (e.g., 3 × 64.98). Restrict decimal division to a single-digit whole number divisor with a multi-digit dividend with up to two decimal places (e.g., 64.98 ÷ 3). The balance of the standard is addressed in Module 4.

9. Examples in this module also include tenths and hundredths in fraction and decimal form.

10. The balance of this cluster is addressed in Module 2. Teach problems such as 2.7 × 2.1 and 4.5 ÷ 1.5. See progressions document, pp. 17–18 (http://commoncoretools.files.wordpress.com/2011/04/ccss_progression_nbt_2011_04_073.pdf).

11. Standard 5.NF.4b is addressed in Module 5. Include problems involving decimal fractions throughout the cluster.

12. The focus of Standard 5.MD.1 in this module is on the customary system of units as a means of introducing fractions (e.g., 1 inch is $\frac{1}{12}$ foot, 1 foot is $\frac{1}{3}$ yard).

13. The balance of this cluster is addressed in Module 4. In this module, Standard 5.NF.4b is applied to multiplying to find volume and area. Standard 5.NF.4b certainly includes decimal fraction side lengths of a rectangle (in both fraction and decimal form).

CHAPTER 6

1. The balance of this cluster is addressed in Module 2.

2. The focus in this module is on the metric system to reinforce place value and writing measurements using mixed units. This standard is addressed again in later modules.

3. The balance of this cluster is addressed in Module 1.

4. Focus on decimal multiplication of a single-digit, whole number factor times a multi-digit number with up to two decimal places (e.g., 3×64.98). Restrict decimal division to a single-digit whole number divisor with a multi-digit dividend with up to two decimal places (e.g., $64.98 \div 3$). The balance of the standard is taught in Module 4.

5. Examples in this module also include tenths and hundredths in fraction and decimal form.

6. The balance of this cluster is addressed in Module 4.

Eureka Math Study Guide: A Story of Units Contributors

Katrina Abdussalaam, Curriculum Writer

Tiah Alphonso, Program Manager—Curriculum Production

Kelly Alsup, Lead Writer / Editor, Grade 4

Catriona Anderson, Program Manager—Implementation Support

Debbie Andorka-Aceves, Curriculum Writer

Eric Angel, Curriculum Writer

Leslie Arceneaux, Lead Writer / Editor, Grade 5

Kate McGill Austin, Lead Writer / Editor, Grades PreK-K

Adam Baker, Lead Writer / Editor, Grade 5

Scott Baldridge, Lead Mathematician and Lead Curriculum Writer

Beth Barnes, Curriculum Writer

Bonnie Bergstresser, Math Auditor

Bill Davidson, Fluency Specialist

Jill Diniz, Program Director

Nancy Diorio, Curriculum Writer

Nancy Doorey, Assessment Advisor

Lacy Endo-Peery, Lead Writer / Editor, Grades PreK-K

Ana Estela, Curriculum Writer

Lessa Faltermann, Math Auditor

Janice Fan, Curriculum Writer

Ellen Fort, Math Auditor

Peggy Golden, Curriculum Writer

Maria Gomes, PreKindergarten Practitioner

Pam Goodner, Curriculum Writer

Greg Gorman, Curriculum Writer

Melanie Gutierrez, Curriculum Writer

Kelley Isinger, Curriculum Writer

Nuhad Jamal, Curriculum Writer

Mary Jones, Lead Writer / Editor, Grade 4

Halle Kananak, Curriculum Writer

Tam Le, Document Production Manager

Susan Lee, Lead Writer / Editor, Grade 3

Jennifer Loftin, Program Manager–Professional Development

Soo Jin Lu, Curriculum Writer

Nell McAnelly, Project Director

Ben McCarty, Lead Mathematician / Editor, PreK-5

Cristina Metcalf, Lead Writer / Editor, Grade 3

Susan Midlarsky, Curriculum Writer

Pat Mohr, Curriculum Writer

Victoria Peacock, Curriculum Writer

Jenny Petrosino, Curriculum Writer

Terrie Poehl, Math Auditor

Robin Ramos, Lead Curriculum Writer / Editor, PreK-5

Cecilia Rudzitis, Curriculum Writer

Tricia Salerno, Curriculum Writer

Chris Sarlo, Curriculum Writer

Ann Rose Sentoro, Curriculum Writer

Colleen Sheeron, Lead Writer / Editor, Grade 2

Gail Smith, Curriculum Writer

Shelley Snow, Curriculum Writer

Kelly Spinks, Curriculum Writer

Marianne Strayton, Lead Writer / Editor, Grade 1

Theresa Streeter, Math Auditor

Lily Talcott, Curriculum Writer

Kevin Tougher, Curriculum Writer

Saffron VanGalder, Lead Writer / Editor, Grade 3

Lisa Watts-Lawton, Lead Writer / Editor, Grade 2

Erin Wheeler, Curriculum Writer

MaryJo Wieland, Curriculum Writer

Jessa Woods, Curriculum Writer

Hae Jung Yang, Lead Writer / Editor, Grade 1

Index

Page references followed by *fig* indicate an illustrated figure.